FAITH IN A
CHANGING
WORLD

FAITH IN A CHANGING WORLD

LESSLIE NEWBIGIN
EDITED BY PAUL WESTON

StPaul's
theological centre

ISBN 978 1 907950 35 3

Published by Alpha International
Holy Trinity Brompton
Brompton Road, London, SW7 1JA
Email: publications@alpha.org
Website: alpha.org

CONTENTS

FOREWORD
NICKY GUMBEL

Bishop Lesslie Newbigin was in his eighties and had begun to lose his sight when he condensed effortlessly from memory his many years of study and reflection into these brilliant lectures. Each talk demonstrates a remarkable lucidity and clarity of thought, always grounded in humility, faith and love.

The talks which form the basis of this new edition combining the 2003 publications *Living Hope in a Changing World and Discovering Truth in a Changing World,* were given at the School of Theology at HTB towards the end of his remarkable life. They demonstrate that he was indeed one of the greatest thinkers and theologians of the twentieth century.

Nicky Gumbel
Vicar, HTB

FOREWORD
SANDY MILLAR

I first met Bishop Lesslie Newbigin when he came one evening to a concert at HTB, which was being given by the New English Orchestra. I asked somewhat diffidently if he would ever be willing to find time to come and talk to us as a church. He instantly and very graciously agreed.

In this way started an association over several years that was of enormous benefit to us, and which led to a warmth and friendship with myself and the church that he was kind enough to express both publicly and privately until his death.

He was involved in world Christianity for well over half a century and, after spending nearly forty years as a missionary in India, instead of retiring to a quiet life in the country, he went to serve in an inner city Birmingham parish.

There was certainly a prophetic anointing on him – for instance, his wisdom and insight in sensing that the beginning of the twenty-first century would see a clash between Western materialism and fundamentalist Islam. And I find it extraordinary to think that in *The Household of God* he so clearly identified the major streams of world Christianity – the Catholic, Protestant and Charismatic – so far ahead of time.

He was such a warm and wise figure. He had such a passion for and commitment to the church. In contrast to the timidity or anxiety of many Christians in the West, Bishop Lesslie's renewed confidence was in the gospel of Jesus Christ and a passionate desire to bring it into the public square. It is of course the story he had come to see as true above all other stories. It is the only story through which humanity and history can be understood. It is the only story that, in its ending foreshadowed in Christ's resurrection, holds out hope for the world. It is the story that had shaped him and in which he lived. It is the story that he brought to life with consummate skill and applied to every aspect of not only church life, but also the wider culture of the world. It is this story that he articulated at our School of Theology between 1994–95, and which forms the basis of this book. 'Here it is,' he seemed to be saying, 'guard it, live it, proclaim it.'

Our hope is that this updated book, including a new introduction by Paul Weston, will inspire many to do just that.

Sandy Millar

Honorary Assistant Bishop in the Diocese of London, and Former Vicar of HTB

INTRODUCTION
PAUL WESTON

I remember very well my first meeting with Lesslie Newbigin in the 1990s when he was already in his mid-eighties. I had returned home from an initial conversation with Professor Andrew Walker at King's College London about the possibility of doing a PhD on Newbigin's work, and he'd suggested that one of the first things I did was to ring the great man. This seemed a rather obvious, but daunting thing to do. But I dutifully looked up 'Newbigin' in the London phone book, and found 'Newbigin, Lesslie'. Must be him, I thought. Not many people spell 'Lesslie' with two 's's, as he did. I found myself ringing the number, and then suddenly began to wonder what I was going to say, should he answer. He did answer, and so I said: 'I'm working on something for a PhD that might interest you.' 'Oh yes,' he replied, 'What is it?' '*You!*' I said, rather too emphatically on reflection. His initial response was one of surprise, but then he added in a friendly self-deprecating tone, 'Well, I suppose I have been known to have a passing interest in myself. You'd better come and see me. What are you doing tomorrow?' 'Nothing,' I said hastily, not wanting to pass up such an opportunity. And so I spent the best part of the following day with him, talking over my project, and starting to get to know a man whom I always found to be generous with his time and still razor-sharp in his thinking. So began a personal 'conversation' with Newbigin which has continued in one form or another ever since, and which has helped to shape my thinking about apologetics, evangelism, and the place of theology in public life.

Around this time, Lesslie Newbigin was regularly invited by Holy

Trinity Brompton to share his insights and his passion for theology and mission, and this book is the combination of two sets of talks that he gave at the HTB School of Theology between 1994 and 1995. Originally these were published as two separate books (*Discovering Truth in a Changing World* and *Living Hope in a Changing World*), but I have rearranged the various chapters in order to make them into one coherent whole. In this new combined volume, you will find the full array of Newbigin's characteristic concerns, expressed in his usual clear, direct and accessible language, but in words that repay attentiveness and serious reflection on the part of the reader.

So, to introduce Lesslie Newbigin to those perhaps unfamiliar with him, there follows a brief biography of him, an introduction to some of the central themes of his writings, and some highlights to look out for as you read through this book.

BIOGRAPHY IN BRIEF

When Lesslie Newbigin died in 1998, his obituary in *The Times* described him as 'one of the foremost missionary statesmen of his generation', and 'one of the outstanding figures on the world Christian stage in the second half of the century'.[1] Most people in Britain who have heard of him will know him because of the impact he made to missionary thinking in the West following his retirement from working in India in 1974. During the following twenty-four years – particularly after 1983 – he gave innumerable talks and lectures, wrote some fifteen books and over 160 articles on the contemporary missionary challenge facing the West (which is itself an inspiring thought when you think that he wrote all this when he was already in his mid-seventies!). But as the obituary points out, he had already come to prominence on the international church scene long before this time, not least as one of the founding bishops of the United Church of South India in 1947, and as a leading ecumenical statesman within the World Council of Churches.

---

1   *The Times*, 31 January 1998.

Early life

Newbigin had gone to India as a missionary in 1936. He had been brought up in the North East of England (being born in Newcastle-upon-Tyne in 1909). Then, after attending a Quaker school in Bath, he had gone up to the University of Cambridge to study geography (and later, economics), where he had revelled in the freedom of thought that he found there. He had also by this time largely abandoned the thought of God as a 'tenable hypothesis', but soon found himself being invited into the friendship circle of the Student Christian Movement (SCM) and kept a semi-open mind about the viability of personal faith, even if as yet he didn't embrace it for himself. A turning point came in his first summer vacation when he agreed to go as a helper on a Quaker camp for unemployed miners in South Wales. It was here that he realised that what the miners really needed was 'some kind of faith' that would strengthen them in the face of 'apathy and despair'. One night – towards the end of the camp – Newbigin experienced a spiritual 'awakening' as he lay on his bed. It came in the form of a vivid picture of the cross of Jesus 'spanning the space between heaven and earth, between ideals and present realities, and with arms that embraced the whole world'.[2]

Returning to Cambridge as a believer, Newbigin's new-found faith began to flourish as he immersed himself in Christian activities. Then at the end of his second year, he reached another significant turning point. Turning down the opportunity to climb with friends in the Alps, he went instead to the Annual SCM Conference at Swanwick in Derbyshire, where he relished the stimulating programme of talks and seminars, and found time to think and pray. During one of these prayer-times, he became absolutely convinced that God was calling him to be ordained, and this changed the course of his life. He spent the next three years working in Glasgow for the SCM, before returning to Cambridge for ordination training at Westminster College.

The opportunity to study theology was particularly significant

---

2   Newbigin, *Unfinished Agenda*, pp. 11–12.

for Newbigin, and it 'profoundly changed and deepened his faith'. He'd arrived in 1933 as a 'typical liberal', but experienced a profound 'evangelical conversion' through studying Paul's letter to the Romans, completing his studies with a strong evangelical conviction about the finished work of Christ on the cross, which was to prove deeply significant for his future ministry.[3]

India

Newbigin departed for India in 1936 newly married to Helen (whom he'd first met at the interviews for the SCM job six years before). She had spent her early years in India, where her parents had been missionaries, and it was natural that Lesslie should have caught her vision to return there. Their ministry in India was to last thirty-eight years (on and off) – until retirement in 1974. He had been ordained by the Presbytery of Edinburgh to work as a Church of Scotland missionary at the Madras Mission, and much of their initial time was spent attempting to master the complexities of the Tamil language. Then, in 1939, they were transferred some fifty miles inland to Kanchipuram (in Tamil Nadu) as district missionaries.

It was during this phase of his ministry that Lesslie became involved in the discussions about a long-running scheme for the uniting of the various denominations in southern India into an ecumenical 'United Church'. In 1942 he was elected to the central committee, and became a fervent advocate of the plan. Five years later – following protracted discussion and debate both in India and back in the UK – the 'Union of the Church of South India' (CSI) was born and was formally established at a celebratory service in Madras Cathedral in September 1947.

It was at this same inaugural service that Newbigin – at the age of thirty-seven – was consecrated as founding bishop of the new diocese of Madurai and Ramnad. He was to serve in this capacity for the next twelve years, endeavouring to be a focus for unity for the varying Christian groups in the area, while making time to

---

3   See Newbigin, *Unfinished Agenda*, pp. 28–29.

visit and evangelise the village congregations under his care, often preaching as many as ten times on a Sunday.

World Council of Churches

It was also from around this time that Newbigin began to be drawn into the work of the World Council of Churches (WCC). He went to its first world assembly in Amsterdam in 1948 as a 'consultant', and was soon co-opted onto the organising committee of the second assembly which was held in Chicago in 1954 (with the theme 'Christ the Hope of the World'). Following this he was appointed vice-chair of the WCC Faith and Order Commission, which set the ecumenical agenda for the third assembly in New Delhi in 1961.

He also became involved with the work of the International Missionary Council (IMC) in promoting the theory and practice of mission and evangelism alongside the more ecumenical work of the wider WCC. In this capacity he was largely responsible for the agenda of its 1952 meeting at Willingen, Germany (on 'The Missionary Obligation of the Church'). So significant was his involvement that he was 'seconded' for a five-year period from his work as a bishop in India to head up the process of integrating the work of the IMC with the wider organisation of the WCC. In 1961 he became the first director of the new WCC division of World Mission and Evangelism and an assistant general secretary of the WCC itself.

Leaving India and the people he had grown to love was not an easy one. There's a touching entry in his diary in which he writes of the great crowd of people who gathered at the station in Madurai to see him off at the close of June 1959. 'At the end,' he says, 'they just stood in a great mass and gazed and gazed at me till I felt I would weep. We sang (a Tamil lyric) and at last the train moved off and the group became only a blob in the distance.'[4] Further down the line, groups of well-wishers had gathered to give him gifts and say their farewells.

---

4   Newbigin, *Unfinished Agenda*, p. 157.

The move ushered in an especially hectic period in Newbigin's life as he juggled a variety of responsibilities – not just in tying up loose ends back in Madurai, but in travelling extensively in his work of the IMC. He visited fifteen countries during a tour of Africa in 1960, toured various centres in the Pacific and Latin America in the following year, and visited the Caribbean in 1962. There were also shorter trips to Thailand, Japan and North America. The Commission had offices in London, New York and Geneva (where much of Newbigin's work was located), but by now the Newbigins had four young children, and so he and Helen decided to set up the family home in Bromley, South London, so that the older ones could attend school in England. On top of all this, he continued to lecture and publish articles and books,[5] and as part of the director's role took on the editorship of the *International Review of Missions*, which involved writing annual editorial surveys of missionary developments around the world.

When the IMC five-year appointment came to an end in 1965, the Newbigins returned to India on Lesslie's election as Bishop of Madras. In a teeming city of nearly three million people (and growing at a rate of 100,000 every year), he was soon immersed in the challenges of the new job, starting initiatives to promote evangelism and outreach, and also developing programmes to help those who lived in the extensive slums that were mushrooming around the city area. He still travelled widely, and continued to be involved in the developing work of the WCC around the world. He was a prominent delegate at the WCC's general assembly at Uppsala, Sweden in 1968, at the Louvain meeting of the WCC Commission on Faith and Order in 1971, and at the Commission on World Mission and Evangelism conference at Bangkok in 1973 (with its theme of 'Salvation Today').

---

5   By 1963 he had already published ten books, and thirty-three shorter articles or book chapters.

'Retirement'

Newbigin 'retired' in 1974 at the age of sixty-five, but seemed to go on finding the energy of someone half his age. Indeed, it could well be said that some of his most significant work was yet to come.

The first thing he and Helen decided to do was to pack some of their belongings into two suitcases and a rucksack and travel across land from Madras back to England (a distance of some 5,000 miles). The whole journey took them two months as they journeyed north from Madras up the central spine of India to Delhi, then to Lahore, across Pakistan, Afghanistan and Iran, before threading the border between Turkey and Russia via Mount Ararat. Then west to Erzurum, Kesari and on to Cappadocia. Each Sunday they tried to find local congregations with whom to worship, but Cappadocia – that strong and vibrant early centre of Christian thought and activity – turned out to be the only place on the entire trip where the Newbigins had to worship on their own because they couldn't find other Christians with whom to share fellowship. This profoundly affected Lesslie and helped to motivate his later critiques of European culture, for it brought home just how completely a once-strong Christian heritage could all but disappear. The journey home continued through Tarsus and the 'Turkish Riviera' to Antalya, then north to Ephesus, Smyrna and Istanbul, before crossing into Europe through Bulgaria, Yugoslavia and Austria, Germany and France.

On arrival back in the UK, Newbigin was invited to join the staff of Selly Oak Colleges in Birmingham in order to teach 'The Theology of Mission' and 'Ecumenical Studies' to students training for missionary work. He also became a minister in the United Reformed Church (becoming its Moderator in 1978–79), and later, in 1981 – at the age of seventy-two – took on the leadership of a small inner-city congregation in Winson Green, Birmingham, which he led for the following seven years.

'The Gospel and Our Culture'

It was during this time that Newbigin's engagement with the

questions facing the church in the West began to take a coherent shape. He had written a short pamphlet arising out of a working party convened by the British Council of Churches which was published in 1983 with the title *The Other Side of 1984: Questions for the Churches*. It soon became a bestseller, and was the first in a series of publications by Newbigin concentrating on the missionary challenges raised by the dominance of an increasingly secularised culture in the West. He was genuinely surprised at how rapidly the questions it raised were taken up by churches across the UK, and later – with typical modesty – described the little book as 'a small blast not of the trumpet but of the tin whistle'. Nonetheless, what became 'The Gospel and Our Culture' programme soon gathered pace and led to two regional conferences in 1990 and 1991 and to an international conference of 400 delegates held in July 1992 at Swanwick in Derbyshire.

In tandem with these public discussions, Newbigin's writings began to focus increasingly on the issues that were being raised by the missionary challenge of the West. A further fourteen books and 160 articles and smaller pieces followed *The Other Side of 1984*, the most well-known of these being *Foolishness to the Greeks* (1986), *The Gospel in a Pluralist Society* (1989), and *Proper Confidence* (1995).

Newbigin's final years were spent in south London where he and Helen had moved in 1992. It was during this period that he became involved with the School of Theology at HTB (which has since evolved into St Paul's Theological Centre, now part of St Mellitus College), and it was as part of this programme of lay education that the material in this book was originally given as talks and lectures.

Lesslie Newbigin died in 1998 at the age of eighty-eight.

CENTRAL THEMES

We move now to consider some of the central themes in Newbigin's writings. Newbigin had already published some seventeen books before his retirement in 1974, and these – arising from his work in India and with the WCC – had already helped to establish him as one of the leading ecumenical missionary thinkers of the twentieth century, long before his return to the UK. Some of the emphases you will find in this book spring out of these earlier reflections and it is worth introducing these themes briefly at this point, before turning to his later thinking about the culture of the West and its missionary challenges.

Trinitarian faith

Newbigin was one of the early champions of the view that Christians really needed to think in Trinitarian terms about their faith, and the first three chapters of this book map this out in some detail. We may take this kind of thinking for granted today, so it's worth remembering that Newbigin's Trinitarian approach to mission was ground-breaking when he first developed it in the early 1960s: so much so in fact that he had to find a publisher outside WCC circles to print his small book *The Relevance of Trinitarian Doctrine for Today's Mission* in 1963.[6] For Newbigin, this Trinitarian understanding continued to undergird his approach to missionary theology.

When you read Part One of this volume, therefore, look for the different ways in which Newbigin draws Trinitarian themes together as a way of describing the dynamic inter-relationships between Father, Son and Spirit. Notice too how the three persons of the Godhead reveal themselves in loving outreach towards the created order, drawing creation itself back into harmony with its Creator once more; and how this eternal and Trinitarian purpose forms the cosmic backdrop to the great work of mission to which we are called as God's people.

Church and unity

Newbigin was deeply committed to the church as the community of faith, and his 1953 book *The Household of God: Lectures on the Nature of the Church* is still a classic in the field of ecclesiology. It is not just a

---

6   Newbigin, *Relevance of Trinitarian Doctrine*. He was later to expand this approach in his 1978 book *The Open Secret: Sketches for a Missionary Theology*.

masterly introduction to the subject, but remains a landmark study because it emphasises the coming importance of the Pentecostal expression of the church alongside the more established Protestant and Catholic patterns of the 1950s. He predicted not only the significance of this newer charismatic stream of church life, but argued strongly that the distinctive emphases of the three traditions were *each* needed to meet the challenges of mission in the years to come.[7]

However, as we have seen from the brief survey of Newbigin's life, he was passionate not just about the church, but about church *unity*, and you will soon pick up something of this passion in the pages that follow, particularly in Chapter 8.

The establishment of the United Church of South India in 1947 was pivotal in Newbigin's ministry, and the struggle for it served to strengthen his life-long conviction about the priority of unity among Christians. He wrote at the time that he was 'so utterly sure that what we are doing is not patching things together, but being led by the Holy Spirit back to the fullness and simplicity of gospel truth'.[8]

The visible unity of the church was not simply an 'institutional nicety' for Newbigin, but an essential expression of the meaning of the gospel itself. As he was later to write: 'a gospel of reconciliation can only be communicated by a reconciled fellowship'.[9] Newbigin fervently believed that only a community of believers visibly reconciled by the atoning work of Christ can properly demonstrate to the world what the good news of God is really all about. And if our churches live in this way, they advertise what heaven – creation restored and reconciled to God – is truly about. As a result, the acquiescence of the church in the face of disunity and separation was an understandably serious matter for Newbigin, and helps to explain why he was such a committed ecumenist to the end of his life. 'The Church cannot abandon this struggle,' he wrote in 1993,

---

7   Newbigin, *Household of God*, p. 111.
8   Newbigin, *Unfinished Agenda*, p. 91.
9   Newbigin, *Household of God*, p. 141.

'without betraying its calling.'[10] For – as he had written nearly twenty years earlier – 'to give up the quest of such unity is to settle for something less than the Gospel'.[11]

The United Church of South India remains to this day a signpost of something profoundly significant but extremely rare in church life: a visible expression of an interdenominational unity in Christ.

How do we know?

Part Two of this book (headed 'Faith and Doctrine') starts with a chapter entitled 'How Do We Know?' This question (a central one in the field of epistemology) was to remain crucially important for Newbigin throughout his life, and his analysis of its implications lies beneath many of the discussions in this book, especially in this particular section.

His first attempt to write about it actually dates right back to an essay entitled 'Revelation' which he wrote as a theological student in Cambridge in 1936.[12] There he discussed the contemporary challenges to the doctrine of revelation, and developed the argument that in contrast to the prevailing assumption that real knowledge must be 'factual' (and therefore somehow 'impersonal'), divine revelation is the living demonstration that *true* knowledge is essentially 'personal': 'we know a person only as he chooses to reveal himself, and only as our own spirit is sensitive and trustful to respond to his revelation'.[13] Approaching the question in this way, the knowledge of God is pictured as a gift of grace imparted to those who would receive it. It is not a piece of metaphysical 'information', but a personal revelation of the loving will of the Creator who longs for his creatures to be known *by* him, and reconciled *to* him.

The question about how we come to 'know' remained important for Newbigin because he believed that Western culture had adopted a number of unexamined assumptions about what could and

---

10   Newbigin, 'Pluralism in the Church', p. 6.
11   Newbigin, 'All in One Place', p. 306.
12   You can find it reprinted in Weston, *Lesslie Newbigin*, pp. 18–21.
13   Weston, *Lesslie Newbigin*, p. 18.

could not be believed as 'true'. Discussions of this theme emerge particularly after 1983 when he comes to address the challenges faced today in the West when Christians try to reach others with the gospel. So a few words on that theme might be helpful in setting Newbigin's later work in context.

The crisis of Western culture

At the heart of Newbigin's later writing (beginning with *The Other Side of 1984*) is a sustained critique of – and response to – the Western church's 'captivity' to the culture of 'modernity' (a term which he discusses on pages 178-81). Within this setting two questions tend to dominate his thought. First, how is the church to communicate the gospel in such a way that it genuinely takes root in the culture to which it is addressed; and secondly, how may confidence in the gospel be recovered when questions of religious *meaning* have been side-lined, and considered merely as matters of private opinion?

In his discussions of these themes (see, for example, Chapters 4–5) the French philosopher René Descartes (1596–1650) and his English successor John Locke (1632–1704) tend to take centre stage. Together, argues Newbigin, they helped to set in place the philosophical assumptions by which the only statements or ideas which can be regarded as really *true* are those which can be shown to be scientifically provable. 'Since Descartes', he writes elsewhere, 'our culture has been dominated by the … search for a kind of knowledge that could not be doubted, a kind of knowledge that involved no risk, no faith commitment. The unquestionable and lucid certainties of mathematics were to provide the paradigm of real knowledge. In the English-speaking world this was powerfully reinforced by the work of John Locke … who defined belief as what we fall back on when we do not have knowledge. Thus "I believe" means "I do not know".'[14]

The attempt to decide the question of truth on such dubious grounds lies at the heart of our cultural malaise, argues Newbigin.

---

14   Newbigin, 'Our Missionary Responsibility', p. 103.

And it leads to a number of distinctions or dichotomies which are still very much in evidence in our contemporary society, each of which tends to divide our lives up into 'public' and 'private' spheres.

'Facts' and 'values'

The malaise becomes clearest, he says, in the distinction we often make between things we commonly accept as 'facts' and those we consider merely as 'values'. 'Facts' are those things that can be established as 'true' by the scientific methods of evidence and proof. Those that don't pass this test cannot be considered 'true', but remain as personal 'choices', 'opinions', or 'values' involving – in theory – a supposed liberty of conscience. So he writes characteristically that 'The public world is a world of facts that are the same for everyone, whatever his values may be; the private world is a world of values where all are free to choose their own values and therefore to pursue such courses of action as will correspond with them.'[15]

The problem of course, is that the scope of the kinds of 'truth' founded on such methods is actually severely limited. It may be able to give answers to a wide variety of mathematical problems, or even establish the structure of the DNA molecule, but in the end it will always remain unable to deal satisfactorily with the most significant questions of human identity and purpose: questions such as, 'Who am I?', 'Why am I here?', or 'For what purpose was I created?' Newbigin addresses some of these questions in detail in Chapters 4, 6 and 10 – particularly in relation to the idea of 'purpose'.

'Knowing' and 'believing'

Closely connected with this distinction between 'facts' and 'values' is the parallel separation between the concepts of 'knowing' and 'believing'. Indeed, there is an inevitable – and related – 'knock-on' effect from one to the other. In the realm of science, Newbigin argues, it is commonly perceived that you can *know* certain things to be true. The educational curricula of our schools and universities

---

15   Newbigin, *Foolishness to the Greeks*, p. 36.

are founded upon such premises: 2+2 = 4; the Battle of Waterloo took place in 1815; and so on. But when it comes to the realm of religious knowledge you can never actually *know* things to be 'true' in the same sense. Judgments in this sphere must stay at the level of the 'subjective', and as far as their 'truth-status' is concerned, can only be considered as 'opinions'.

So while the theory that the cosmos began with a 'Big Bang' is accepted as a 'fact', any suggestion that the Bible may be right in positing the existence and involvement of a Creator in the act or process of creation can only ever have the status of an extra-curricular 'opinion'. As Newbigin puts it in *The Gospel in a Pluralist Society*: 'We are pluralist in respect of what we call beliefs but we are not pluralist in respect of what we call facts. The former are a matter of personal decision; the latter are a matter of public knowledge.'[16]

'Reason' and 'revelation'

Summing all this up, Newbigin sets these kinds of distinctions in a wider philosophical, cultural, and *spiritual* framework. He argues essentially that the central flaw in the culture of the West is that it has reduced meaningful knowledge – as the gift of a personal God – to that which is 'proof-based' and therefore depersonalised. As he puts it, 'The "Age of Reason" supposed that there was available to human beings a kind of indubitable knowledge, capable of being grasped by all human beings which was more reliable than any alleged revelation, and which could therefore provide the criteria by which any alleged divine revelation could be assessed.'[17]

By so doing, the relationship between revelation and reason in the West has effectively been inverted: divine revelation is rejected, and human reason is enthroned as the sole arbiter of truth – both human and divine. And in the process, the knowledge of God the Creator of all – though properly 'public' – is reduced to the realm of the 'private'.

---

16   Newbigin, *Gospel in a Pluralist Society*, p. 27.
17   Newbigin, 'Religious Pluralism', p. 233.

THE MISSIONARY CHALLENGE

Not surprisingly, Newbigin presents the missionary challenge facing the contemporary church in stark terms. 'The Church', he writes, 'is not generally perceived as concerned with facts, with the realities which finally govern the world and which we shall in the end have to acknowledge whether we like them or not.' Consequently, as long as the church is content to 'offer its beliefs modestly as simply one of the many brands available in the ideological supermarket, no offence is taken'.[18] But to claim more than this is something which will remain culturally unacceptable.

So what is Newbigin's response? In a sense I want to leave you to read what follows in order to answer that question. But by way of introduction perhaps two brief points may be helpful.

First, the name Michael Polanyi crops up in Chapter 4, and then again at the start of Part Three (pages 172–74). This Hungarian chemist-turned-philosopher is a key figure in helping Newbigin to explain his response to the challenge. Polanyi wrote an important book in the 1950s called *Personal Knowledge* which deeply influenced Newbigin, and in which he set out as a scientist to show that 'complete objectivity as usually attributed to the exact sciences is a delusion and is in fact a false ideal'.[19] All knowing, he argued, begins with some kind of unproven (and un-provable) *faith*-commitment: a sort of personal intuition about the nature of reality which forms the starting point out of which fresh discoveries can be made. The important point for Polanyi is that at this formative stage in the process of discovery, a kind of personal *trust* is exercised: trust in a view of reality which forms the basis for further thought and action, even though it cannot yet be proved to be true.

In effect, Polanyi's approach to the question of 'knowing' cuts right across the accepted 'enlightenment' model with its emphasis on the objectivity and superiority of 'reason'. Newbigin happily finds in this insight a way of re-establishing a broader conception

---

18   Newbigin, *Gospel in a Pluralist Society*, p. 7.
19   Polanyi, *Personal Knowledge*, p. 18.

of knowing, and uses Polanyi's idea of 'personal knowledge' to defend the idea that our knowledge of God – though inescapably *personal* – is nonetheless *real* knowledge, and therefore opens up the possibility of talking once more about the truthfulness of *religious* knowing.

Second, Newbigin's response to the missionary challenge of the West is that this proper and genuine knowledge of God through Jesus in the power of the Spirit is made visible in corporate form *through the church*. Indeed it is in and through the ongoing life of believing congregations that a renewed grasp of genuine reality is made evident and intelligible to others. It was in this vein that Newbigin wrote the following words back in 1989, which provide a fitting way to conclude this introductory chapter:

> *I have come to feel that the primary reality of which we have to take account in seeking for a Christian impact on public life is the Christian congregation. How is it possible that the gospel should be credible, that people should come to believe that the power which has the last word in human affairs is represented by a man hanging on a cross? I am suggesting that the only answer, the only hermeneutic of the gospel, is a congregation of men and women who believe it and live by it.*[20]

So read on. I am confident that you too will find yourself challenged, inspired and invigorated by one of the most significant missionary thinkers of our time.

---

20   Newbigin, *Gospel in a Pluralist Society*, p. 227.

BIBLIOGRAPHY

Newbigin, Lesslie, 'All in One Place or All of One Sort? On Unity and Diversity in the Church', in Richard W. A. McKinney (ed.), *Creation and Culture: Studies in Honour of T. F. Torrance*, Edinburgh: T & T Clark, 1976, pp. 288–306.

—— *Foolishness to the Greeks: The Gospel and Western Culture*, London: SPCK, 1986.

—— *The Gospel in a Pluralist Society*, London: SPCK, 1989.

—— *The Household of God: Lectures on the Nature of the Church*, London: SCM Press, 1953.

—— 'Our Missionary Responsibility in the Crisis of Western Culture' (1988), reprinted in Eleanor Jackson (ed.), *A Word in Season: Perspectives on Christian World Missions*, Grand Rapids, MI/Edinburgh: Eerdmans/Saint Andrew Press, 1994, pp. 98–112.

—— 'Pluralism in the Church', *ReNews [Presbyterians For Renewal]* 4, No. 2, May 1993, pp. 1, 6–7.

—— *The Relevance of Trinitarian Doctrine for Today's Mission*, C.W.M.E. Study Pamphlets, No. 2, London: Edinburgh House, 1963.

—— 'Religious Pluralism: A Missiological Approach', in *Theology of Religions: Christianity and Other Religions*, Rome: Pontifical Gregorian University, 1993, pp. 227–44.

—— *Unfinished Agenda: An Updated Autobiography*, 2nd edn, Edinburgh: Saint Andrew Press, 1993.

Polanyi, Michael, *Personal Knowledge: Towards a Post-Critical Philosophy*, Chicago: University of Chicago Press, 1958.

Weston, Paul, ed., *Lesslie Newbigin, Missionary Theologian: A Reader*, London/Grand Rapids, MI: SPCK/ Eerdmans, 2006.

PART ONE

FAITH AND THE TRINITY

1 GOD THE HOLY TRINITY

The Bible Society has translated the Scriptures into hundreds of languages, and it is intriguing that they all have at least one word to express the idea of God. No matter how vaguely conceived, it appears that every language has a word – usually many – to symbolise a sense or form of reality that is beyond ourselves.

I often recall the day I spent with a primitive hill tribe in the forests of Southern India. They lived in caves. The government had built them houses but they preferred not to live in them; it was not their way. One of them took me to the top of their mountain to show me his cave. Without a guide you would never have found the caves because they were so skilfully concealed.

We talked all that day of many things, and I asked, 'Who do you think made us all?' He replied without hesitation, 'Kadavul'. This was one of the many Tamil names for God. It became obvious that despite their having had no contact whatever with Christianity, nor with what we call Hinduism, their language and culture were inextricably connected to a notion of God.

So this sense of the reality of God is universal, except when it has been suppressed, as in our own culture, by a strange and perhaps passing fashion of thought. But of course, the word has a curious variety of meanings. In Madras, the city in which I spent the first seven years of my life as a missionary, there is a temple. In one part of the temple, there was the teaching of Ramanuja, the great theistic philosopher of the eleventh century, who taught a most remarkable doctrine of God based upon the ideas of grace, sin and forgiveness. In another part of the same temple, cobras were worshipped as God.

India, above all, is the home of what one might call the natural religions: those which do not claim any special revelation from God but which see God in some sense in everything. The whole of reality is permeated by this presence. God is not to be understood as someone who has actually made his own nature known to us beyond doubt. God is beyond human knowledge. The human condition is not to be understood by looking at historical events but rather on the model of nature. Everything that we know in nature moves in a cyclical way, from birth through growth, maturity, decay and death and then the birth of a new animal, a new child, a new leaf – everything moves in a circle.

The planets appear to move around us. The earth revolves around the sun. Empires, civilisations and philosophies rise, mature, decay and fall – that is the natural way of understanding our human situation. This is the way the great religions of Asia broadly understand it. God is beyond all these events in this passing, changing world. In one of the most fundamental doctrines of the great Hindu classics it is affirmed that God is 'nirguna', that is to say, 'without qualities'. You cannot describe God in any way. You cannot say anything about him. He is beyond human thought.

In contrast there are the three great religions known as the religions of the book: Christianity, Judaism and Islam. They all claim to be based upon God's revelation in history. They look at historical events and claim that at those points God made himself known, so that we cannot just waffle about him, so to speak. He has a definite character: he is like this and not like that.

The ancient classical world into which Christianity was born was in one sense simply an extension of Asia, because that is what Europe was, and the philosophy and the popular religions of that classical world were of the same family as those of Asia, certainly those of India. But within that classical world, there was a community apart. In all the great Greek cities there would be a synagogue, a place where this strange nation of Israel, which refused to accept the general religious beliefs of the society and refused to worship any of its gods, remained the people of the God of Abraham, Isaac and Jacob. They were a people who had received from God the Torah, which we translate as 'law', but which is not so much a legal system but rather a divine guiding and directing.

If you want to understand what the Torah means, immerse yourself in Psalm 119 where the psalmist, in those long passages, meditated on, delighted in and expressed his love for the guiding, teaching, warning, disciplining hand of God. So the people of Israel were a sort of non-conformist society in that classical world, sometimes admired for the purity of their monotheistic faith, sometimes despised, often hated because they did not conform. They remained a kind of pointer beyond the natural religion that surrounded them towards the reality of a God who was not 'nirguna' but who had a definite character, who was the Creator of all things, so that nothing existed except by his grace and permission.

Everything was ultimately under his rule. But he was also the God of the covenant, the God who in his pure grace and kindness had made a covenant – first of all with the whole human race in the story of the flood that we read in Genesis 9 – the covenant whose sign was the rainbow. God had pledged himself to the human race; he had said that he would not cast them off. God was therefore a God who directed, guided, warned and disciplined.

We often misrepresent the God of the law when we start the Decalogue with the words of the commandments, instead of beginning them, as is recorded: 'I am the Lord your God, who brought you out of the land of Egypt. Therefore you shall have no other gods but me.' One misconstrues the first commandment if one does not see it as the second part of a sentence of which the first part is pure grace. It is as the God of grace who has rescued his people and made a covenant with them that he warns them not to worship other gods and not to do all those things that would involve forsaking him. In creation, covenant, discipline, God is both the God of wrath and the God of love. These two are not opposed to each other but are on the opposite sides of the same coin. God's love for us is so great that our turning away to seek other gods can only provoke his wrath – a wrathful love and a loving wrath.

Here was a God with a definite character. I have lived a long time in India and have listened to people use the term 'god' much more freely than in the West. You then realise the difference between a kind of vaguely conceived idea of a god, who is really beyond our knowledge, and a clear, definite, formidable, inescapable character who is made known to us when we live with the Scriptures. The Scriptures are the rendering of his character because they are the story of his mighty acts.

So we have these synagogues in the cities of the ancient classical world. Into the synagogue at Antioch there came those two formidable figures: Barnabas and Paul. It was the beginning of a tremendous explosion which was to bring out of the synagogue that world faith we call Christianity. If you try to put yourself into the position of a Jewish worshipper, listening to the message that Paul and Barnabas brought, you will see they were certainly not preaching a new religion. They were telling you that the thing you had longed for, prayed for and believed in, had happened – or had begun to happen.

The Jewish people had been formed by this covenant of a gracious God, a God who had given the Holy Land to them. He had promised them that though he would punish and discipline them and scatter them because of their sins, in the end he would restore them to the Holy Land. He would make them a blessing for the whole earth, scattering their enemies and putting them under their feet.

If God was God then he must fulfil his promises. If he did not, he was not God. The Israelite community in those pagan cities knew that the Holy Land was being desecrated and trampled on by the heathen and that they themselves were scattered throughout the world but continued to read Sabbath by Sabbath the great promises of God. It was unbelievable for them that God should not in the end fulfil his promise and therefore they lived in that tremendous tension of hope.

So here was a man who told them that God had acted to fulfil his promise, but not as they had expected. Rather, God's way seemed to many almost unbelievable because it appeared incompatible with their sense of what God's salvation must be. What Paul, Barnabas and the other apostles did in synagogue after synagogue was to ask their Jewish listeners to study the Scriptures again, to look at them afresh in the light of what had happened in Jesus Christ: the Old Testament showed that God had warned his people in generation after generation. He had punished them, disciplined them, sent prophets to remind them of their calling to be his salvation for the whole earth, to be a light to the Gentiles, and they had rejected those prophets, persecuted and killed them. God himself, speaking through the prophets, had spoken of his own agony: 'How can I cast you off, O Ephraim? My heart is torn within me' (Hosea 11:8).

We see the agony of God as his wrath against his people struggles with his faithful love for his people. So Paul and Barnabas asked those Jewish people to read the Scriptures again and realise that it was in suffering that the grace, mercy and glory of God had been revealed to them. That long story was brought to a climax and the Messiah himself had come and suffered. So, for example, the great prophecy in Isaiah about the servant of the Lord who bore the sin of the world had now been fulfilled in the actual life, death and resurrection of Jesus Christ.

The confidence that God would raise the holy dead was an integral part of the eschatological hope, the messianic hope of the Jewish people. Though earlier parts of the Old Testament do not seem to hold out hope of anything like resurrection, it seems to have emerged during the period of the great Maccabean wars[21] when many thousands of Jews, rather than fight on the Sabbath day, perished for the sake of God's law. The strong belief arose then

---

21   During the second century BC.

that in the end God could not forsake them: they would be raised from the dead to share in the joy of God's victory. Any suggestion of resurrection would therefore immediately evoke the tingling sense that this must be the beginning of the new age, of the new creation.

There were also Old Testament prophecies of the pouring out of the Spirit of God upon all flesh as the sign that the new age had come. And that is what had now happened. So when Paul and Barnabas told the congregations in the synagogues in Iconium, Lystra and Derbe to read their Scriptures again, it was with the intention of helping them understand that God had now acted to fulfil the longing that was at the very heart of their faith. But it was not in the sense they expected – that they would destroy their enemies and return to reoccupy the Holy Land. Instead it was by a movement in the opposite direction. From Israel would go forth the reconciling word of God, which would fulfil the purpose for which God called upon Israel, and of which the prophets often spoke: 'You shall be a light to the Gentiles; you shall be my salvation to the ends of the earth.' These apostles were stating a new and given fact, not some new idea or some new religion. God had so acted that if you truly understood your Scriptures, you would understand that the new age had dawned and that the new creation had begun.

Who was this Jesus about whom they spoke? He was a man who felt and suffered as all humans do. But he was also the one who at the outset of his ministry was acknowledged by the Father as his Son and anointed by the Spirit of the Father. His baptism marked the manifestation of his reality as the one who was the Son of the Father and through whom the Father poured out the Holy Spirit upon his Son and upon those whom he gave to his Son.

If you have not already done so I would recommend your reading one of the Gospels right through at a sitting and then allowing the picture that this creates to sink into your mind, to allow the total reality of Jesus as we are shown him in the Scriptures, to be etched into your mind.

Jesus manifested the power of God in the mighty works he did.

He made clear the authority of God in his teaching. He quoted from the Torah: 'You have heard that it was said to them of old times ...' But then went on: 'But I say to you ...' Not, of course, to destroy the Torah but to bring it to its fullness, to its completeness. In everything he did and said, he spoke not on his own authority, but as the one sent by the Father. Everything was in reference to the Father. He did not, like a conquering son of David, set out to bring the world under his control. That was the temptation of the devil in the wilderness after his baptism.

He was the obedient, loving Son of the Father, who was the sovereign over all the world. It was by his loving obedience to the Father in every situation confronting him that he showed what it meant to say that God was sovereign. In other words, he manifested in his own person the kingship of God, the kingdom of God, which was the very heart of his message. It was as the Son that he manifested the Father and we have glimpses into the intimacy of his continuing relationship with the Father, for example in his anointing by the Spirit with the power of the Father to heal and to teach.

So it was not a new religion: it was the fulfilment of the hope of Israel. It was, if you like, the new Exodus, the new Passover or even more fundamentally the beginning of the new creation. And, therefore, everything about our understanding of God had to be thought through afresh in the light of what had actually happened in the ministry of Jesus.

It is fascinating to look where the Greek writers of the Gospels fall into Aramaic when they quote Jesus. If you have lived, as I have, in a place where everybody speaks another language – in my case Tamil – then you will understand me when I say that even if I am speaking English, there are certain experiences or words I have encountered which I just think of in Tamil because that is how they were given to me. The sounds are still in my mind. And when you hear an English-speaking Tamil giving a speech, you will notice how every now and then the speaker drops into Tamil because it is something so deep in the heart.

And so it was on the rare occasions when the Greek writers of the Gospels quoted Jesus in the Aramaic language that he spoke. Two particular words were always on the lips of Jesus and constantly repeated in Aramaic. One is *Abba*, Father. Not the Greek word but the intimate Aramaic word that a child would use for 'father'. It is a word that opens a window into the very heart of Jesus, and reveals the intimacy of his relationship with the Father.

The other word is *Amen*. It is usually translated 'verily' as in, 'Verily I say unto you'. No one else, as far as we know, had acquired the habit of using *Amen* at the beginning of a sentence: 'Amen I say to you'. It is a solemn word deriving from the Hebrew root which means 'absolute faithfulness and reliability'. Jesus seems to have been unique in using this word as a preface to his momentous sayings. It expresses total authority, an absolutely faithful rendering of the truth. Take those two words together – *Abba* and *Amen* – and you have a light penetrating the very heart of Jesus. On the one hand, he spoke as no other human being has ever spoken or could speak – with the direct authority of God – but on the other hand, he had this childlike intimacy with the Father.

What does one make of that? How does it affect the way one thinks about God? Obviously it took a long time to work out the implications, though the New Testament is full of phrases which refer to the Father, the Son and the Holy Spirit and, if you look below the surface, you will find over and again in Paul's letters this threefold reference. But, it was a long time before the full implications of this could be worked out because it was such a revolution in thinking as to what the word 'God' meant.

The story is fascinating. I always regretted that when I was a theological student and had to study all the heresy of the first four centuries, nobody really explained to me that it was all part of the struggle to express the new reality that had come into the world with Jesus, using the old language which was already saturated with Greek philosophical thought and with the strict monotheism of the Old Testament.

Finally the church was led to see that God was not a single monad in the sky, not a super-human or a super-person. So when we use the word 'God' we refer to something which perhaps we can only speak of as a communion of love – a communion of love forever given and forever enjoyed. If God was a single person, then how could we say that God is love because we could only think of it as love unrequited, because there would be nothing pre-existing the creation for God to love. To put it in a more truly biblical way, if we learn from Jesus what it means to speak of God, we shall know that we are speaking of that communion of love which exists between the Son and the Father in the bond of the Spirit. We are not speaking about love unrequited but of love forever given and forever enjoyed – the communion of love – and therefore the primal reality that lies behind all that which exists is this communion of love and joy in the life of the Godhead.

The whole creation is not just the product of an arbitrary will but the overflow of an immense love, that out of the communion of love which is the being of God, there has been given a world which could reflect that love and a human family within that world, which could return that love. This makes an enormous difference to how you understand the word 'God'.

We must ask how far – at least in Western Christianity – our understanding of God has been truly Trinitarian. When we use the word God in ordinary speech, to ordinary people, do any of us think of the Trinity?

I often remember the time I went over the ruins of Fountains Abbey in Yorkshire with my wife and her sister. At each point where we looked at some part of the old building, there was an explanatory paragraph in the guide book. When we reached the ruins of the Chapter House, the following appeared in the guide: 'Here in the Chapter House the monks gathered every Sunday to hear a sermon from the Abbot except on Trinity Sunday, owing to the difficulty of the subject.'

Why was the subject difficult? Obviously, because the monk had inherited, and deep down in his mind there remained, an essentially unitarian picture of God. One could spend much time discussing the origin of that picture. Much of it, I think, came from what is called 'natural theology', from the kind of philosophical exercise of seeking to prove the existence of God on rational grounds from the rest of human experience. And of course the God who is thus produced is not the blessed Trinity, but something else.

However, for the ancient classical world, the doctrine of the Trinity came not as a puzzle but as its solution. The ancient classical world, rather like ours, was losing both its nerve and confidence by the time we arrive at the third and fourth centuries. Jesus had been born in the reign of Augustus when the classical world was at the zenith of its glory and confidence. But by the third and fourth centuries, that confidence had evaporated, partly because there were problems the classical world could not solve.

The first puzzle was the relationship between what the Greeks called the intelligible and the sensible or what we call the spiritual and the material. It seemed to them that there was an absolute dichotomy between the material world which forms our history and with which we deal every day, and the mental, spiritual world of ideas, which for Plato was the real and ultimate world. If Plato was right, reality was merely a shadow. However, from the point of view of someone living in this material world, Plato's world of ideas might itself be seen as a shadow. That dichotomy, that split or dualism between the spiritual and the material, meant that the two could never really meet and that for practical purposes this material world was all we had to go on.

The other great unsolved puzzle arose from the relationship between what the ancients called 'virtue' and 'fortune' – between whatever skill, courage, intelligence and cunning a person brings to the struggle of life on the one hand, and ineluctable fate on the other, which confronts and in the end always destroys that human being. So that human life even at its bravest and most heroic is finally a losing battle against the ineluctable, irresistible power of fate or fortune – the goddess Fortuna.

Those two dichotomies could not be solved within the worldview of the ancient classical world. When the church had developed that new model, that new way of understanding reality in terms of the Father, the Son and the Holy Spirit, the puzzle could be solved. The power that ruled over all things, which the pagans called 'fate', and the spirit that moved within a human being to meet it, were one in the man Jesus who went on his way from Bethlehem to Calvary. And the invisible spiritual world, the invisible spiritual universal principle which holds all things together, the *logos*, had become the actual human being Jesus Christ who is part of history and whom we can know, see, hear and listen to. So a new model for understanding the whole human situation was provided and it was from that power, out of the ruins of the classical world when it was overwhelmed by the Barbarian invasion, that a new civilisation could arise based upon the biblical story understood in terms of the Trinitarian doctrine of God. So now it was not a puzzle but the solution to a puzzle.

What are the implications for our Christian discipleship? I suggest two: the first is that it changes our whole worldview and our understanding of what it is to be human. We are familiar, as was the ancient world, with models of the human situation based on the idea of struggle and violence. In the background of the Old Testament there is the pagan myth of the primeval conflict where the dragon is murdered and the world made from its corpse. It is a primal myth where violence is seen as the origin or basis of human life. In our own time, through various supposed implications of Darwin's theory of evolution, there is the idea that human life is to be understood as a power struggle in which the weakest go to the wall and the survivors, because they are stronger, survive.

This appears to be very deeply rooted in the mind and is one of the unquestioned assumptions of our own time about how the world is. It explains the gratuitous amount of violence on television which occupies so much of our waking hours, especially those of children. The doctrine of God as Trinity gives us a completely different picture of what the ultimate meaning of human life is. It means that the primordial reality from which all things come, and to which all things are directed, is that shared communion of love and bliss which is the being of the Trinity. This makes an enormous difference to the way we understand the human situation, which is the final primordial reality.

What we see in the New Testament, or rather in the Bible as a whole, is a picture that contradicts that myth. I think we have to say that a great deal of our Christian thinking has not been fully Trinitarian. For example, the creation story in Genesis is so often read as if it was simply the sheer command of a solitary potentate, while in contrast the New Testament teaches us that the world was created by the triune God: Father, Son and Holy Spirit. The New Testament speaks a great deal about the role of Christ in creation and the Genesis chapter itself, of course, speaks of the role of the Holy Spirit in creation. So that we see creation not just as a matter of God's command, but as the overflowing of his love. The creation is a gift of God's love and, as Calvin reminds us, it is intended to be 'the theatre of his glory' where the glory of God, which is the love of God, is to be reflected and manifested.

It is wholly significant that only in recent years has attention been drawn to the first chapter of Genesis that speaks about our being made in the image of God and explicitly states that it is as male and female that we are made in that image. Much Christian history relies on the assumption that it was as male that we were made in the image of God. So in all the great discussions among theologians about what it means to assert that we are made in that image, it has been man's reason (and I use the word 'man' here deliberately) and his power of reasoning, and therefore his power over the created world, which represents God's image in us.

The book of Genesis affirms that it is as male and female that we are created in the image of God. That is a reminder for us that built into creation from the beginning is the love which binds a man and woman together and which is truly the reflection of God's love. Therefore, at the very heart of our understanding of creation it is not primarily the idea of power, or even reason, but rather the love of God shared with us so that we might reflect and embody that love in the whole life of creation.

So that first implication is really about the whole worldview, or if you like, the story by which we understand our lives. I think one cannot escape the fact that the story by which people understand their lives in our society is struggle for survival, where the strong prevail over the weak. That notion is deep within our thinking and this Trinitarian understanding of God contradicts this and affirms that the primordial reality from which all things come, and to which all things are intended to converge, is the communion of love given and enjoyed, the bliss of the Holy Trinity.

The second application, or implication, to which I would like to refer concerns how we come to know God through prayer and meditation.

I think all human beings pray at some time or other. But what are we doing when we pray? Are we simply projecting our desires on to the universe hoping that there is someone there to answer? I am often moved by that passage where we read of Jesus praying in a certain place and afterwards his disciples say to him, 'Lord, teach us to pray.' That picture is of Jesus in his intimate childlike communion with his Father with the disciples standing around knowing they do not know how to pray and going to Jesus, saying, 'Teach us to pray.'

Jesus told them, 'No one knows the Father, except the Son and any to whom the Son is willing to reveal him.' We do not know God as Father without Jesus. We are accustomed to end our prayers with the words: 'Through Jesus Christ our Lord.' I sometimes wonder how much meaning there is in those words. If we start our prayers from that picture of the disciples watching Jesus at prayer and then saying, 'Lord, teach us to pray', it will mean that our prayers will always be, whether we say it or not, 'through Jesus Christ our Lord'. As we come to know Jesus better, as we give time day by day to soak ourselves in the words and deeds of Jesus so that he becomes 'our eternal contemporary', then it will follow that in our prayers, we are seeking to pray with and through Jesus, so it is the communion of Jesus with his Father into which we are drawn. It is the prayer that Jesus offers to his Father that we make our own, and we do it only because Jesus himself has given us of his Spirit. We share in the same Spirit where Jesus is one with his Father.

The other relationship where it seems to me that the teaching of the Trinity is so important is in our public worship. This is the worship of the Father through the Son in the power of the Spirit. It is the only right way for us to offer our worship. We are not ourselves fit for the worship of God, but insofar as Jesus has made us his own through the work of his Spirit, we are able as a corporate body, as a family and a church, to become part of the prayer of Jesus. The Epistle to the Hebrews states that Jesus 'is at the right hand of the Father ever pleading for us'. So our prayers are not simply our efforts projected into an empty sky. Instead, we are taken up into the praying of Jesus, which he is forever offering to the Father. We have something to learn here from the Eastern Orthodox Church. If you have attended worship in such a church you will know that people go in and out all the time. You can never tell when the service begins or ends. From an Orthodox point of view that would be an absurd statement because in their view you are just dropping in on the eternal worshipping life of the Trinity.

An Anglican friend was on holiday in Crete and went to church one Sunday morning. He did not know that he was going to have to stand for three hours. The priest observed that after about an hour and a half he was beginning to become a little restive, and he beckoned to the deacon. He whispered some words and the deacon went out and ten minutes later returned and went to where my friend was standing and told him, 'There is a poached egg in the vestry.' My friend replied, 'But the liturgy?' To which the deacon responded, 'The liturgy is eternal. The egg will get cold!' From his point of view there was no harm in going out and having a poached egg and coming back again. Worship is not primarily our thing. To say that it starts at 10.30 and finishes at 12.00 is absurd. It is our dropping in to the eternal worship of the Holy Trinity. That is why in an Orthodox church you will see children running in and out all the time and no one is in the least disturbed. They are simply participating in that eternal worship which is the very life of the

Trinity. As we know from the great consecration prayer in St John's Gospel, the purpose of our Lord's atoning death is that we might be made one with the Father and the Son in their eternal communion of love. That is the source from which all things come and that is the goal for which all things, and all of us, are made.

2 JESUS THE INCARNATE SON

How should we speak of Jesus? He is the light of the world, as the sun is the light of our earthly world. We do not try to look at the sun. We have to turn away when we try, but it is because of the sun that we see the world. How then do we look at Jesus?

One thing still holds good, whether people are believers or unbelievers, Jesus has a fascination. A constant stream of books appears about Jesus, some of them helpful, some not. Many of them claim to tell us who Jesus really was in contrast to the Jesus that the church talks about.

In a sense one can understand this because our Christian creed passes over the actual life of Jesus with hardly a mention. If you remember, the creed runs: 'Born of the Virgin Mary, suffered under Pontius Pilate, was crucified, dead and buried.' There is no word about the actual life and ministry of Jesus. And that of course creates the danger that people will think of Jesus simply as a sort of cipher or factor in a theological equation.

In the eighteenth century the intellectual leadership of Europe turned away from the Christian faith and adopted a new faith, the faith of rational secularism. At the same time, there was a new understanding of history. After the Enlightenment, history was seen in a different way because the doctrine of progress, which was born in that period, caused people to look at the past in a quite different way. So people began to ask, 'Well, who was the real Jesus? Not the Christ that the church preaches and talks about, but who was this actual man? What sort of man was he?' The quest was for the so-called 'historical Jesus', or the Jesus of history. Hundreds of books have been written, claiming to give us a picture of Jesus as he really was and not as the church presented him.

In one sense this is just a typical example of hubris. When I talk about Jesus as he really was, I really am talking about Jesus as he seems to me, in contrast to all the others who simply do not understand! C. S. Lewis has a nice little phrase on 'chronological snobbery'. We assume that because we are of the twenty-first century, we consequently understand things better than those of the past, even those closest to Jesus. And so there has been this quest for what was called the 'Jesus of history'.

What are our sources? What can we know about Jesus? Our sources, of course, are all of them (with one exception that I shall mention) written by people who believed that Jesus was Lord and Saviour and believed in the resurrection. The earliest sources are the Epistles of Paul and the other apostolic writers. We should never forget that these were the first. Their writings are the earliest material we have. Some of them were written with certainty within a decade or two of the resurrection. From these Epistles we do not get a detailed account of the life of Jesus but we do get an account of who Jesus was and what he now means to us.

And then there are the Gospels. In one sense they date back to the earliest times because they are based on stories people told about Jesus. But in their present form they are later than the Epistles. We have to remember that the Christian gospel went rapidly in all directions from Jerusalem and most of it was spread by people unknown to us. The three great churches of the early centuries – Alexandria, Antioch and Rome – were all founded by people we just do not know. Among these founders were people who fled from Jerusalem to avoid persecution but were not apostles, or by missionaries who were simply Christians spreading the gospel and talking about Jesus.

In these and other centres, memories of Jesus accumulated from the stories recounted by those people who had first come and given the good news. Gradually these narratives were gathered together with various churches having different collections. The effort was later made to bring these collections together and to put them into a more orderly shape and from this we have our four Gospels: Matthew, Mark, Luke and John, each of which differs somewhat from the other. They have a great deal of material in common, but each has its own character, because they come from different circumstances and embody the memories of disparate groups of people.

For some people these differences are worrying. If you are in contact with Muslims you will know that they hold this as a charge against Christians. In contrast there is the unambiguous Koran with no doubt about any of the words in it. The four Gospels, however, give somewhat different accounts of what took place. There is hardly any saying or deed of Jesus that has not come down to us in different versions. The Muslims interpret this to mean that we have lost the real Gospel, the *Injil* as they call it, and therefore the New Testament cannot be trusted.

But as we know, if in a lawsuit all the witnesses for one side gave identical evidence, then we would suspect the lawyers of implanting ideas in them. It is a character of a real historical event that it tends to be reported in varying ways according to the interpretations and perceptions of different people.

In the Gospels we have material from many different memories and sources and we must remember that this material is far closer to the actual event, and therefore much more reliable than anything we have in relation to the rest of the world of the first century. The first manuscripts we have of events such as Caesar's *Wars* come centuries after the earliest manuscripts of the New Testament. So we can say that the evidence given to us for the actual happenings recorded in the Gospel is far stronger than anything we have for any other part of the world of that time.

All these documents were written by people who believed Jesus was the risen and reigning Lord, the one we praise in our prayers. There is one ancient reference to Jesus by the Roman historian Tacitus. In describing riots in Rome during the first century he records that Christians were suspected of causing the disturbances. Christians, he reported, were a 'pestilential sect of people' who believed that somebody called Christ, who had been executed as a terrorist by the Roman governor, was still alive.

That is the only other contemporary, or nearly contemporary, record we have of Jesus. That is what really happened, according to Tacitus. Of course, we have to make up our minds which is the true understanding of what really happened: that one, or the one given to us in the testimony of the apostles.

To attempt to understand the life of Jesus we have to begin, I think, by trying to understand the world into which he came. Imagine yourself as a devout Jewish believer, a child of Israel, living then in what we now call Palestine. Behind you are all the promises of God: the great story of the Exodus, the liberation, the settlement of the land, the giving of the Promised Land to the people, the sins of Israel, the punishment, the dispersion, the scattering to Babylon, Assyria and all over the place, the holy people scattered, the Holy Land desecrated, pagan Roman armies trampling over the Holy Land, the Temple destroyed and only recently rebuilt with Roman approval, but the Holy Land still desecrated by pagans.

Then there were all those promises of God that he would restore his people to the land, make them the great ruling nation of the world, scattering their enemies and putting them to shame. Every page of the Old Testament is full of those promises. But what happened? What was God doing? If God was simply leaving things like that, then he was not God. If you were a devout child of Israel then you had to believe that God was going to intervene, that somehow or other God was going to manifest his sovereignty over all the world and put his enemies to flight. So there was this tingling expectation running through the whole life of the nation.

As in any human society, there was within it a variety, a spectrum. At one end of this society's spectrum were the priests and the

Sadducees. In India, the ruling British government left small princes in charge of local areas just as the Romans did. They made Herod a puppet king under their ultimate control and permitted the rebuilding of the Temple to make the Jews happy. The company of priests, the Sadducees, of which the priests were the central core, were accommodating and making do. In Jerusalem they accepted the status quo and ceased to expect any dramatic intervention.

Then there were the Pharisees who took their religion far more seriously. They cooperated, attended the Temple and took part in the Temple worship. But they believed that the real clue to the future was that Israel should be faithful to the Law, and therefore the synagogue, where the Law and the prophets were taught and studied and where people were encouraged to live exactly according to that Law. That was the way in which one could fulfil God's purposes and prepare the way for his coming.

And then there was a third group represented by what we call the Qumran documents, discovered in 1947 in the caves of Qumran. They came from a sect which rejected both the Sadducees and the Pharisees. The Pharisees were rejected because they were cooperating too easily with the Sadducees and the Sadducees because they were cooperating with Rome. They had formed this community in the desert to wait and pray for the day when God would intervene and scatter his enemies.

Finally, at the other end of the spectrum, there were the zealots or terrorists and revolutionaries, who believed that the only way to fulfil God's purpose for Israel was to take up arms and drive out the Romans, hoping that God would support them in doing so just as he had supported the Maccabees two centuries earlier.

So there was this spectrum, but throughout the whole of society there was this tingling expectation. I have called it a smouldering volcano. Every now and then a spurt of flame would come out. Small intermittent terrorist uprisings occurred, many of which were put down ruthlessly by the Romans. It was reported that so many people were crucified that the Romans ran out of wood for crosses. But as Jesus warned in so much of his teaching, unless

Israel repented, the volcano would erupt and there would be a mighty disaster. That, of course, happened in AD 70. There was this final great revolt which the Romans crushed, thereby destroying the Jewish state, reducing Jerusalem to a pile of rubble.

It is into such a society that Jesus came. And we should remember that first of all, as we know from the Gospels, Jesus was acknowledged as a rabbi. A rabbi was not a member of a professional class like a modern clergyman. He was a layman who had studied, understood and mastered the Scriptures so he could be a teacher of others. It is significant that Jesus was constantly addressed by the Pharisees and others as a rabbi. So during those years he lived in Nazareth he was not just doing the work of a carpenter. In fact, we do not know whether he was one at all. But he was certainly studying the Scriptures and possessed such deep insight into them, and mastery of them, that he was recognised as a rabbi.

What triggered the beginning of the public ministry of Jesus, as we know from all the Gospels, was the coming of John the Baptist. All the sources agree about that. John the Baptist appeared after centuries during which there seemed to be no prophet. After Malachi the people of Israel moaned and groaned that there was no prophet. But here God had raised up someone who was the authentic voice of the Lord, who spoke as the prophets of old had spoken, calling Israel to repent and return to their God. So there was this great movement of repentance, of coming to be baptised afresh – as it were – to make a new start. And the news of this came to Jesus in Nazareth. He heard it as the call of his Father and he came with the crowds to be baptised. Our first sight of Jesus in his public ministry was of his coming as one of a crowd of sinners seeking repentance. Here we have already what we speak of when we say that Jesus took upon himself the sin of the world. He made no distinction between himself and others. He came asking for baptism along with a company of sinful men and women. As we know, John would have restrained him, but Jesus replies: 'No, this is how God wills it to be.'

At his baptism there is that decisive moment when he is

acknowledged by the Father as, 'My beloved Son' and then anointed by the Holy Spirit for the start of his ministry. There we have the beginnings of what has become the doctrine of the Trinity.

Immediately Jesus is driven into the desert to wrestle with the awesome question: 'How does the Son of God act in practice?' There was that great struggle in the desert where Jesus mastered all the powers that could tempt him away from the Father's will. And when he completed that great inner spiritual battle and emerged victorious, he returned to Galilee and began to preach the message: 'The kingdom of heaven is at hand. The kingdom of God is at hand.'

What does that mean? It was not news to a Jew to say that God was King, because that was the whole message of the Old Testament. What did it mean to say that the kingship of God, the sovereignty of God, was at hand? It meant that a kingship of God was no longer something in the distant future, or something in heaven, or a kind of theological topic for discussion, but something confronting you here and now.

The kingdom of God, the reign of God, the sovereignty of God, the sovereign power of God is here and now, confronting you, meeting you, but you cannot see it because you are looking the wrong way. So turn around. The Greek word *metanoein* translates as 'repent', which means to make a mental U-turn, to look the other way. This is because you are looking in the wrong direction when you say, 'God is king.' You are expecting a different thing. That is not what God is. Turn around, repent and follow. And some of them did with excitement and enthusiasm. But then they began to ask: 'Where is the kingship of God? We don't see it.' And Jesus answers with parables and stories. If you examine those stories you will see that all of them in fact tell the story of Israel but in a new way, subverting Israel's own story.

I could give a dozen examples, but just take the parable of the wicked landowner (Matthew 21:33–41). The parable of the vineyard in Isaiah was one of the best known parables of the Old Testament. Israel was the vineyard. God planted the trees there to bring forth fruit and he gave it to tenants, to Israel, to his own people, but they failed to give the fruit he asked for and so he sent servants, the prophets, but one after another the people rejected them. So finally he would send his only Son, and what would they do to him? They would kill him. And what would the owner do? Bring the tenants to a wretched end. The Pharisees who heard that quite clearly understood what it meant and that is why they looked for a way to arrest Jesus.

All these parables retell the story of Israel but tell it with a new ending, and the new ending is in the person of Jesus himself. But many people do not understand. When the disciples went to Jesus saying they were puzzled, they were told, 'The secret of the kingdom of God has been given to you ...' (Mark 4:11) but to others who are not, it is simply a mystery, a miracle. And then there are what the first three Gospels call the 'mighty works' and what the fourth Gospel calls the 'signs'. These were acts of power through which the mastery of Jesus over all the powers of evil was demonstrated, but never as a means of attracting attention.

Jesus told the people not to talk about his miracles. They were simply the outworking of the love of God. One of the most beautiful examples is at the beginning of Mark's Gospel when a leper comes and kneels before Jesus and says, 'Lord, if you are willing, you can make me clean.' And Jesus simply replied: 'I am willing ... Be clean' (Mark 1:40–41). He touched him, and laid his hand upon him. It was a sheer act of the love of God, not part of a missionary strategy, but a sheer act of God's love and power. But once again, the miracles had a sharp cutting edge. They divided people. You remember John the Baptist asking, 'Are you the one who is to come or do we look for another?' And Jesus said, 'Look what is happening: the blind see, the deaf hear, the lame walk, the dead are raised up. And blessed is he who is not caused to stumble' (Luke 7:20–23).

For some people the miracles were not a revelation of the presence of God; they were something else. First of all, of course, the mission of Jesus was to Israel. He told his disciples to go nowhere except among the lost sheep of Israel because his first calling was to summon

Israel to be as God had created it to be. Jesus would be his servant who would suffer. He would bear the sin of the world. The vision that we have, in Isaiah 53, is of the servant of the Lord, there on behalf of all nations, to bring the true knowledge of God to them, by bearing the suffering which comes at that meeting point between a holy God and a sinful world. Jesus sought to call upon Israel to fulfil that for which God had called Israel into being. But Israel would not listen. There were many warnings of what would come if Israel did not repent, and it eventually came in AD 70.

It became clear that God's purpose for Israel had to be fulfilled in one alone. Jesus himself must be the one who suffered for the sake of the world. Accordingly he prepared his disciples for what was to come, and part of it was the promise of resurrection at the end. One of the great thoughts of the time, certainly in the minds of the Pharisees and those looking for the redemption of Israel, was that there would be a resurrection of the dead. From the time of the Maccabean wars onwards it was believed that those who had died for the sake of the Lord would be raised to life.

Therefore resurrection was a fundamental hope and belief. As we know from the Scriptures, the Sadducees did not accept the hope of resurrection. They were perfectly comfortable with things as they were. They did not need a resurrection in their settled world. But the hope of resurrection was a sign that you did not accept the world as it was, but that you looked for a radically new one.

So Jesus prepared his disciples for what they could hardly bear to have heard: that his mission must end in failure, and that he must suffer on behalf of all. But he also gave them the promise of resurrection. Jesus went forward with utter confidence in his Father. And those two Aramaic words to which I have previously referred, we still hear in the original Aramaic. Those who heard those words could never forget them. The writers of the Gospels wrote in Greek but they uttered those two words in the original Aramaic: *Abba* – Father, and *Amen* – Truly. 'Amen, Amen I say unto you.' These words uttered a confidence in his Father that nothing could shake, a confidence which enabled him to go forward in absolute faith and obedience to what was, from a human point of view, not merely death but also the total failure of his mission and the impending disaster for which he had prepared and warned his hearers.

Inevitably he went alone to Gethsemane and to the trial and scourging, the mocking and the crucifixion – and the extraordinary prayer: 'Father, forgive them' (Luke 23:34). And the verb in that prayer is a verb that means repeated action. At each hammer blow, as the nails were driven into his body, Jesus exclaimed, 'Father, forgive; Father, forgive; Father, forgive; Father forgive.'

And then we hear that terrible cry: 'My God, my God, why have you forsaken me?' The beloved Son was torn from the Father. The beloved Son had so totally identified himself with a fallen world, cut off from God, that he shared in the desolation of that fallen world.

Now when we begin to speak about these things, we are compelled to remember that the cross of Jesus is ultimately a mystery that we can approach but never penetrate. The cross of Jesus is the decisive encounter between a holy God and a sinful world. It is the point where the one true crisis of all cosmic history occurs. We can never fully penetrate what it means. If we could understand it then we could explain evil and if we could explain evil it would not be evil.

If you look at the earliest writings in the New Testament, you will see that the first way in which the cross of Jesus is spoken of is as a mighty victory: 'Now is the judgment of this world; now shall the prince of this world be cast out' (John 12:31). The death of Jesus is a mighty victory. It is the power of God and the wisdom of God. And if you look at the early representations of Jesus in the first few centuries in icons and so forth, you will never see the drooping pain-drenched figure of a medieval crucifix. You will always see the figure of a man with his head erect, beating down the power of Satan. That is the first picture of the cross we get both from the New Testament and from the earliest iconography.

But then, of course, we are bound to ask, 'How has evil been conquered? How has the enemy been put to flight?' And there we have to turn to the many different metaphors that the New Testament uses, all of which help us but none of which completely explains.

There is the metaphor of a ransom: Jesus rescued us from the power of evil. But if you push that too far there are these questions: To whom was the ransom paid? Was it paid to God or to the devil? There were great arguments about that in the Middle Ages.

Take the concept of substitution: Jesus died in our place. That is true. Jesus died for sinners. He took, as Paul said, 'the likeness of sinful flesh for sin' (Romans 8:3). But it was not a substitution which left us behind. It was not as if Jesus did something for which we could then say, 'Thank you very much, that's okay.' Jesus did something so that we may follow him and with him go by the way of the cross. He did what no other could do, but he did it not so that nobody else should, but that all should follow in his steps.

Then there is the concept of sacrifice, so much developed in the letter to the Hebrews. This is indeed the one true, full, perfect and sufficient sacrifice. It is the consummation of all sacrifice, but again one has to ask, 'Why should God require sacrifice?' To answer this it seems to me that we have to go into the very heart of the whole scriptural testimony, where in the Old Testament we see the agony of God. In the book of Hosea, chapter 11, God says: 'How shall I give you up, O Ephraim? How can I abandon you? My compassions are struggling within me.' There is an agony in the heart of God between the holiness of God and the love of God. We realise that God is holy with a holiness that can make no compromise with evil, and that God is love, with a love that can never give up the evildoer. So there was this agony in the very heart of God and the crucifixion of Jesus was, so to speak, the actual working out of that agony within this history of ours.

I am, of course, struggling with something too deep for any human being fully to grasp, because I am persuaded that the cross of Jesus is the ultimate turning point in all human history and all cosmic history, and we can never pretend to have it wrapped up in a neat formula. But at least, it seems to me, one way to look at it is to realise, as I have said previously, that we need a Trinitarian understanding of God if we are to understand the cross. It was by the will of the Father, Son and Spirit, that the Son was torn from the

Father's breast to become part of a world which had turned its back on the Father and become alienated from him. So that right there in history, in the middle of this fallen human history, in our fallen world shut off from God, there was the actual presence of God in the form of sinful flesh. As Paul said, he came as part of our world, and yet as the very presence of God himself.

We know this because Jesus rose from the dead. The Father honoured the obedience of the Son and raised him from the dead. That resurrection cannot fit into any theory of the world based on some other foundation. The resurrection can only make sense if you begin with it. It cannot be part of any understanding of the world, except as an understanding which begins from the resurrection. This is because the resurrection, like the creation, was an utterly new beginning. We know that it was a bodily resurrection because the tomb was empty. If there was one clear thing about the evidence, it was that the tomb was empty. But on the other hand, the body of the risen Jesus was not like our physical bodies, which cannot go through closed doors: it was the foretaste of the new creation, the new heaven and the new earth for which we look.

It is the pledge and the foretaste, the sign that what happened on Calvary was not the defeat of God's love but its victory. And this secret was shared. It was communicated to those men and women he had prepared to be its bearers. They knew that despite the situation here in history, where evil triumphs and good suffers, nevertheless the final victory was with God. The church was called upon to carry through history that for which Jesus suffered on the cross.

And that is why when Jesus assembled his frightened disciples, he said, 'As the Father has sent me, so I am sending you' (John 20:21). He showed them his hands and his side, the scars of the Passion, the wounds that come through bearing the sin of the world. They would be the marks that identify the church as the body of Christ. And then he breathed upon them saying, 'Receive the Holy Spirit' (John 20:22).

As Paul reminds us in Romans 8, the Holy Spirit of God groans within us because the Holy Spirit is given to us that we may share in the Passion of Christ for the world, so that our little sufferings and groanings are taken up into the great groaning of the Holy Spirit. The church was called upon to carry through history that bearing of the sin of the world, so that Jesus could say to them, 'If you forgive the sins of any, they are forgiven them; if you retain the sins of any, they are retained' (John 20:23 NKJV). The church now becomes the place where this forgiving, reconciling, atoning work of Jesus is carried on through history, so that the church is that place where anyone can be given the possibility of being reconciled to God through the atoning work of Jesus.

I know that to speak about the cross is to talk of something more than any human formula can encompass. We need all those metaphors that Scripture gave us: ransom, substitution, sacrifice. We need them all to help us understand the central truth within the cross. As Paul says, ' ... the power of God and the wisdom of God' were at work (1 Corinthians 1:24). In this way we are able to understand that here is the place where evil is finally defeated.

That is the Jesus of history. The Jesus of history is the Christ of faith. This quarrel that has gone on among theologians for the past two hundred years is based on a false presupposition. It is not that there is a Jesus of history whose life we can write as thousands of writers have tried to do, on the one hand, and the Christ of faith, on the other hand, whom we worship and adore in the church.

There is only one Jesus. He is the one we read about in the New Testament. The so-called Jesus of history is simply Jesus looked at from the point of view of a faith other than the Christian faith. It is Jesus looked at from the point of view of the rationalism of the Enlightenment. It is no more than that. The one Jesus who is the Jesus of history is also the Christ of faith. He is the one Lord, and there is no other.

3 LIFE TOGETHER IN THE HOLY SPIRIT

It is at the very heart of our gospel that in the public life of this world God has acted. This, as I have said, contrasts with both the dominant assumptions of Asian religion and of much religion in the West, where religion is seen essentially as a private and inward matter and therefore a matter of the individual relationship between the human soul and God. That is certainly the typically Asian, and classical form, of religion.

The view is taken that God is not to be found in actual events of history but to some extent by the exercise of our reason and partly by opening ourselves to spiritual experiences of various kinds. It is in contrast to this that in the gospel we proclaim historical facts, which are part of the public history of the world, to be evidence of God taking his decisive action in the world.

But of course if we stop there, then Jesus would simply be a figure of the past whom we might admire and might seek to follow – but he would still be someone in the past. Let us now consider the work of the Holy Spirit through whom we are made contemporaries with Christ, or Christ is made our contemporary. The faith that we proclaim, and this life that we live, is anchored in a historic deed under Pontius Pilate. That phrase in the creed always reminds us that we are talking about something in the public history of the world by naming the Roman governor of that time. We are anchoring our confession of faith in actual events of history. But in so doing we are not simply revering something in the past. It is an acknowledgement that God's Holy Spirit has made Christ our living contemporary and made us his contemporaries, being participants in his continuing life.

It is the Trinitarian understanding of God which alone enables us to make sense of these realities. So when we speak of God we refer to the Father, the Creator and Sustainer of all things, whose providence rules over all the events of history, though often it is hidden from us. And when we speak of God, we speak of the Son, who became incarnate at a particular time and place in the public history of the world, and of the Holy Spirit, uniting us to Christ. The Holy Spirit unites us to the Son and to the Father, so that our faith, while it is anchored in a real event in history, at the same time it is a continuing, living, inward communion between our spirits and God himself.

The Holy Spirit is the Spirit of Jesus. The New Testament constantly reminds us that this is the test. There are many spirits in the world. 'Spirituality' is now a vogue word. A friend of mine says that whenever he hears that term he wants to reach for his gun, and I understand why! There are many weird things going around under the name of 'spirituality'. St Paul tells us that the test, the mark of the Holy Spirit, is the confession that Jesus is Lord (Romans 10:9). In the first letter of John, it is put even more sharply: 'Jesus Christ has come in the flesh' (1 John 4:2). That is the test of the Spirit, not some Jesus that we invent or picture in our minds, but Jesus come in the flesh: this actual human being, Jesus. That is the test that this is truly the Holy Spirit.

Let us look at some of the great biblical teachings about the Holy Spirit. We start, of course, at the very beginning where the Holy Spirit is active in creation, brooding over the chaos. Throughout the Old Testament, the Holy Spirit is at work in the prophets and great heroes of the faith, inspiring their words. Then we come to the one who is, in a sense, the last link in the chain of prophets, John the

Baptist. He came like one of the old prophets to call Israel back to her Lord. He offered a baptism of repentance, bringing Israel, as it were, back to the starting point to begin again, to repent and to be blessed by God. And John, as we know, promised, 'I baptise you with water, but one more powerful than I will come ... he will baptise you with the Holy Spirit and with fire' (Luke 3:16).

So Jesus came seeking that repentance, that conversion of Israel for which John the Baptist was calling. Jesus humbly accepted that baptism in water followed with an anointing by the Holy Spirit, and was declared to be the Son of God, the beloved. So at that point the baptism in water and the baptism in the Holy Spirit came together. Jesus accepted the baptism in water, and immediately afterwards he is anointed in the power of the Holy Spirit.

We read then that the Spirit drove him into the wilderness for those days of struggle and temptation when Jesus had to face these questions: 'If you are the Son of God, what will you do? How will you show your power? How will you exercise God's power?' In that mighty struggle, of which Jesus spoke in some of his parables, he tamed the power of the enemy and came forth from the desert in the power of the Holy Spirit to proclaim the reign, the kingdom and the sovereignty of God and went through the villages and towns of Galilee and Judea performing those miraculous acts which the Holy Spirit made possible.

Time and again he reminded them that it was the Holy Spirit who was active in his great works. But as St John tells us quite plainly (John 7:38f) the Holy Spirit was not yet given because Jesus was not yet glorified. Jesus was anointed with the power of the Holy Spirit and in that power he spoke those words and did those deeds. But the Spirit was not yet given to others. It was not given to the disciples because Jesus was not yet glorified. He had not as yet accomplished that final atonement, that final act of reconciliation through which it would be possible for the Holy Spirit to be poured upon the believers.

We remember in the fourth Gospel the farewell addresses to the disciples at the Last Supper. Jesus promised in different ways that the Holy Spirit would come, though he himself would be leaving them. In John 14 he speaks of the *paraclete,* one who is called to stand beside you. It can mean an attorney or advocate. In a lawsuit an advocate stands beside you to plead your case. In that sense the Holy Spirit was the one who would be the presence of Jesus for them when his visible fleshly presence was no longer with them.

Then at the end of that chapter it is written that he 'will teach you all things [so that you may understand the fullness of the truth] and will remind you of everything I have said to you' (John 14:26). Towards the end of chapter 15, after speaking of the rejection and persecution the church must face, we have these words: 'When the Counsellor [Comforter] comes ... he will testify about me. And you also must testify, for you have been with me from the beginning' (John 15:26–27). But it was the Holy Spirit who was the primary witness and that must never be forgotten. The Holy Spirit is the primary witness, the Counsellor, the *Paraclete* and the Comforter. When we use the term Comforter we have to be careful because the modern meaning implies something soft and cuddly. But the original meaning of the word 'comfort' is reminiscent of steel. Comfort was the strength and power that the Holy Spirit would grant the disciples.

In chapter 16 Jesus says the Holy Spirit will convict the world in respect of sin, righteousness and judgment. In other words, the Holy Spirit would prove the world wrong in its fundamental ideas. In that sense the Holy Spirit could carry forward the work of Jesus. Above all, the death of Jesus revealed that the wisdom and power of God were manifest in the weakness and foolishness of the cross.

God had judged all human wisdom, righteousness and power, and that judging, convicting work of Christ would be continued by the Holy Spirit. When the Holy Spirit was present, people would be forced to realise that even their fundamental ideas of sin, righteousness and judgment were wrong. They had to be completely rethought. That is the meaning of repentance. It means a radical change of mind. So the Holy Spirit would convict the world in respect of sin, righteousness and judgment.

Secondly, the Holy Spirit would bear witness to Jesus. He would remind the disciples of all that Jesus had said and done. 'He will guide you into all truth ... he will speak only what he hears, and he will tell you what is yet to come. All that belongs to the Father is mine. That is why I said the Spirit will take from what is mine and make it known to you' (John 16:13, 15). That promise was at the very heart of the mission of the church. Jesus had said to them, 'I have much more to say to you, more than you can now bear' (John 16:12). That little group of first-century Palestinian fishermen could not grasp the fullness of God's truth. How would it, or could it, be grasped? As they went out in the power of the Spirit to take the gospel to all the nations, the Spirit would show them the fullness of what it meant that Jesus was, and is, Lord.

This, I believe, is fundamental to our apologetic. It is as we bring the light of the gospel to bear on every human situation that we find that this light, so to speak, comes back and we discover more fully the meaning, glory and power of Jesus. As the church goes out into all the nations on its missionary task, the Spirit will show that all the Father has belongs to Jesus. The whole range of human knowledge will not take us beyond the reality of Jesus. 'All that the Father has is mine, therefore, I say, he will take what is mine and show it to you.' This is a marvellous 'authorisation' for what might be called the cultural mission of the church.

As the gospel is brought into every culture, the Spirit shows how everything belongs to Christ. And as the church goes on this pilgrimage it shows how the light of Christ illuminates and enables us truly to understand the whole of cosmic reality: 'All that the Father has is mine, therefore, I say, he will take what is mine and show it to you' (John 16:15).

So far I have been following St John's account. This of course leads up to the moment in the upper room when Jesus, after showing them his hands and side, said, 'As the Father has sent me, I am sending you. And with that he breathed on them and said, "Receive the Holy Spirit"' (John 20:21–22). This would empower them for their message.

In Luke the story is told differently. Remember that at the beginning of Acts, the disciples went to Jesus, saying, 'Lord, are you at this time going to restore the kingdom to Israel?' (Acts 1:6) And Jesus replied, 'It is not for you to know the times or dates the Father has set by his own authority. But you will receive power when the Holy Spirit comes on you; and you will be my witnesses in Jerusalem, and in all Judea and Samaria, and to the ends of the earth' (Acts 1:7–8).

The question the disciples asked was about the kingdom: 'Will you restore the kingdom?' After all, this was the message of Jesus: 'The kingdom of God has come.' It had looked as if the devil had won on the cross. But now, in the light of the resurrection, they knew that the cross was indeed victory, not defeat. So when do we see the kingdom? Do we not see it now? Is now not the time? It is a question we constantly ask: 'Lord, when will you show us your power?' It is a natural question. And the answer of Jesus came in the form of both warning and promise. There is this warning: 'It is not for you to know the times and seasons which the Father has set in his own authority.'

It is sometimes annoying when people ask me whether I am optimistic or pessimistic about the future of the church. The only reply is that I believe Jesus rose from the dead and therefore the question does not arise. It is not a human programme. It is bearing witness to God's kingdom. It is not whether one is an optimist or pessimist but rather whether or not one believes. That is the question. So Jesus warned them, 'It is not for you to know the times and seasons.' It was the Father's kingdom. It was not their programme. 'But, when the Holy Spirit comes whom the Father will send, he will bear witness and you will be my witnesses to the ends of the earth.'

What is the connection between the question ('Will you restore the kingdom?') and the promise of the Holy Spirit? The answer, as the whole of the New Testament shows, is that the Holy Spirit is the foretaste of the kingdom. There is a beautiful Greek word *arrabon*, which is translated in our different versions as 'pledge' or 'guarantee' or 'promise'. It puzzled scholars for a long time because it is not a word of classical Greek. Then early in the twentieth century many sheets of papyrus were discovered under the sands of Egypt upon which this word *arrabon* was frequently written. It was discovered that these were the accounts of shopkeepers and that *arrabon* meant a sum deposited in promise of payment.

An Egyptian student told me the word is still used. If you want to buy a shirt in a Cairo shop you decide on the style of the cloth and the tailor then asks you to make a deposit as a pledge to pay when he has finished. That is called an *arrabon*, and this is the word used for the Holy Spirit. It is the foretaste, the pledge or down payment. It is not just an IOU, but real cash for the thing itself. But it is not just that real thing, it is the fact that this 'cash' carries with it the assurance of the full amount to come. This is the wonderful word the New Testament uses in many places for the Holy Spirit. The Holy Spirit is the pledge of the kingdom, not just a verbal promise or an IOU. It is a prelude to, a real foretaste of the power and love of God, given to us now. But it is such that it holds out a promise for the future.

It is rather like going to one of those posh dinner parties – to which, incidentally, I seldom get invited! – where one is kept standing around talking and wondering if there is ever going to be anything to eat. You then hear a tinkling sound and a drinks trolley is brought in. You are jolly glad to have the drinks, and it is very refreshing, but more important is the suggestion that something is cooking, and at last you are going to get a meal! The Holy Spirit, you see, by association, is the aperitif for the kingdom! It is a real gift of the love, power and glory of God. But it is such an extraordinary gift that there is more. It is the promise, the assurance that there is the full glory, complete power and infinite wisdom of God to be revealed, and that is what makes us witnesses in the true sense of that word. It is the Holy Spirit who is the witness because that presence assures us, and can be the assurance for others, that the glory of God is a reality to which we can look forward.

On the day of Pentecost that promise was fulfilled. The disciples, together in one place, received this blessing and the flame descended on their individual heads so that it was both a corporate gift to the whole body, binding them together into one, but also a deeply personal gift to each, bringing the very power and presence of Christ into their personal lives. And then, as the book of Acts continues, we see how the Spirit empowers the apostles for their mission to the nations.

If we go on to Paul we see in 1 Corinthians that he encountered difficulties with a church that prided itself on its spiritual gifts. Factions resulted and disputes arose as to which gifts of the Spirit were most important. In those wonderful passages in chapters 12, 13 and 14, Paul used the body to explain, by analogy, how the Spirit worked. 'For we were all baptised by one Spirit into one body' (1 Corinthians 12:13). So the baptism of water and the baptism of the Holy Spirit were one. The baptism by which we are made one is baptism in the Spirit. It is the one Spirit who enables the body to become a body.

But a body is only corporate if its members are different from one another. The difference is what makes the body corporate. Neither noses nor pairs of eyes constitute a body, so if one asserts that noses are best then that is an expression of absurdity. And that was Paul's complaint against the Corinthians, that their particular spiritual gifts were supposedly the best. Paul went through a great list. There were different lists in different letters, in Romans and Ephesians, in Colossians and Corinthians, because the gifts of the Spirit could not be catalogued completely. But the point Paul made was that all those gifts were given for the sake of the body, so that each part might minister to its whole.

Then comes that incredibly beautiful language celebrated in chapter 13: 'If I speak in human or angelic tongues, but have not love, I am only a resounding gong or a clanging cymbal. If I have the gift of prophecy and can fathom all mysteries and all knowledge, and if I have a faith that can move mountains, but have not love, I am nothing' (1 Corinthians 13:1–2). There follows that wonderful description of what love is, that lifeblood which enables the different limbs and organs of the body to work in harmony, as part of the whole. If that blood should cease to flow then both limb and organ would die. And so love was the supreme gift of the Spirit because it ensured and made possible this harmony.

In chapter 14 Paul gives much sound practical advice on the different gifts found in the life of any congregation. One could speak of other passages of Paul, especially that superb piece in Galatians 5, when he spoke of those wonderful fruits of the Spirit: love, joy, peace, patience, kindness, goodness, faithfulness, gentleness and self-control.

Perhaps the greatest chapter in the Bible on the Holy Spirit occurs in Romans 8, and I could speak and write interminably upon its beauty. It begins by telling us we have been put under a new jurisdiction, a new regime: 'You were under the law of sin and death, but now, by what Christ has done by dying for us, Christ coming in the likeness of sinful flesh, we have been brought under the rule of the Spirit of life in Christ Jesus.' There has been a change of regime, of jurisdiction. We have been transferred from one jurisdiction to another and are now under the rule of the Spirit of life in Christ Jesus. Again, in verses 8–17 we see that the Spirit is a pledge. If the Spirit of God is given to us, then the Spirit will also pour life into our mortal bodies. The Spirit is the pledge of resurrection. Though we are now all part and parcel of this sinful world, there is the pledge of the total redemption of the body, of resurrection from the dead.

The Spirit then enables us to call God, 'Father'. When we say, *Abba*, Father, it is that Spirit which makes this possible. When we also, like Jesus, use that word and call Jesus 'Father', in the way that Jesus called God 'Father', it is again the work of the Spirit who enables us to do that. This is the mark of the Spirit because it is the Spirit of Jesus and the Holy Spirit uniting us with him so that in, and through, and with Jesus, we speak of God as Father, *Abba*, Father.

And if we are children, then we are heirs – heirs with Christ. In other words, children may not look very important, as they are.

They may be small and weak, but if they are the heirs of a great estate then there is something more than just weakness and smallness. The Christian may seem a weak, small and insignificant thing in the life of the world but the Spirit convinces us that we are heirs. If we are the children of God then we are the heirs of his kingdom and we can look forward to its full riches. Once again, the Spirit is the pledge that assures us of the fullness to come.

But then Paul immediately states that this is authentic on one condition, that we suffer with him. If we suffer with him, then we shall be glorified with him. That would be the mark. Jesus had breathed upon them, saying, 'Receive the Holy Spirit.' He showed them his hands and his side, the scars of the Passion. So the mark of the authenticity of our confession, *Abba*, Father, the mark of our true union with Jesus, would be that we suffer with him, so that we may be glorified with him. We are with Jesus always at that frontier which divides the kingdom of the rule of God from the rule of the devil, that place where hourly and daily the war is waged between two kingdoms, two regimes. If we suffer with him we may be also glorified with him.

From verses 18–27 Paul picks up that theme of suffering, saying that it is not just we who suffer but the whole of creation. All creation is groaning and travailing in pain. We do not need to be told that. Creation is full of pain, suffering and frustration, but Paul says, 'These are the birth pangs of a new creation.' That is the meaning of this suffering and the Holy Spirit assures us of that. The Holy Spirit is the foretaste, pledge, the *arrabon* of a new creation.

We who have already received the first fruit of the new creation, the Spirit, groan within ourselves, waiting for our adoption. And the Spirit himself helps us with groanings that cannot be uttered. So the Spirit who is the Spirit of Jesus, the Spirit of the crucified and risen One, the Spirit of the One whose body was marked with the scars of the nails, this Spirit is with us as we groan in travail. And we do so with the assurance that these pains are the pains of childbirth, because a new creation is being born. As Paul said, 'For in this hope we were saved' (Romans 8:24).

And therein lies this nice concatenation whereby hope looks to the future. Our salvation is in the past: something already done. But we are saved in hope. It is never that we are saved and that is that – everything is fine and there are no problems. No, our past salvation moves ever forward, and is the hope with which we approach the present and the future. We are saved so that by the presence of the Spirit, we may also participate in this great struggle for the new creation, following Jesus on the way of the cross and having the Spirit, the Spirit of Jesus with us, who unites his groanings with ours and assures us that we are indeed the children of God. It is absurd to discuss this briefly because one could spend hours on it. So I commend to you the study of Romans 8, the richest chapter in the whole Bible about our life together in the Spirit.

Finally, I return to where I began. It is by the presence of the Spirit and his work in our lives that Jesus, crucified under Pontius Pilate, the Jesus of history, is for us the Christ of faith. It is the Holy Spirit who is the Spirit of God and the Spirit of Jesus, who makes Jesus our contemporary, so that we have this intensely inward and personal reality of communion with our Lord Jesus Christ in the power of the Spirit. So in this sense the historical factuality, the public factuality of the gospel – incarnate, crucified under Pontius Pilate, risen – is united with the immediacy, the inwardness of our life with Christ in the power of the Spirit. It seems to me tremendously important to hold this together – the historical, given factuality of the gospel and the inward, personal and continuing life of the soul.

In a sense all that I am saying is summed up in the acclamation we offer at a certain point in the Eucharist: 'Christ has died, Christ is risen, Christ will come again.' Christ has died, that is a fact. It is the great basic historic fact: we are not just talking about an inward and personal experience which has no way of being publicly verified but about the fact that Christ died. But then Christ has risen. The risen Lord Jesus Christ, in the power of the Spirit, is our eternal contemporary and we are now able to converse with him, to listen to him and follow him, to have a life of personal communion with him until he comes again. And Christ will come again, and the more we go on in our inward devotion to Jesus in our personal interior lives, the more we long for the day when we shall see him face to face.

And it is the Holy Spirit who gives us this assurance because we have already received the pledge, the *arrabon*, the foretaste of the Spirit. That is what makes us witnesses and what fills us with hope in the midst of our pain and struggling. That is what enables us to know that the Jesus whom we know now through the Spirit, we shall, at the end of the day, see face to face. Thanks be to God.

PART TWO

FAITH AND DOCTRINE

4 HOW DO WE KNOW?

Because Part Two of this book is about Christian doctrine we should perhaps start by looking closely at the whole business of how do we 'know'?

Many people think the Christian faith is not something you 'know' but only something that you 'believe'. In our culture, knowing and believing are supposed to be different from each other. So, this is the point where we should make a start.

In our present culture there is a strange belief that doubt is somehow more honest than faith. This belief suggests that faith might lead you astray, and that doubt is the mark of an honest inquirer. This, of course, is nonsense. Both faith and doubt have proper parts to play in the business of knowing. But faith is primary.

You cannot know anything unless you begin by believing. This beginning means opening your eyes, trusting the evidence of your senses and being aware of a world beyond yourself. We can only begin to 'know' something when there is this initial act of faith.

We might later come to doubt some of the things we first believed. We cannot believe everything, but doubt is only possible on the basis of something that we believe. I could make a statement and you might doubt its truth. I could then ask you why you doubted it, and you would reply, 'Because I believe something else.' I could follow this by saying, 'But I doubt that.' There is no rational doubt except on the basis of faith. So faith is primary and doubt secondary.

One of the consequences of this contemporary fashion, of regarding doubt as more honest than faith, is that it leads to a profound conservatism. This is because in every society there is what sociologists call a 'plausibility structure'. There exists a whole pattern of beliefs that in general nobody questions. It is taken for granted that this is how everything is and everybody knows and accepts the situation. If something is proposed which seems to contradict that plausibility structure, then we doubt it. So when doubt is put primarily above faith it means that we tend to accept what everybody else believes. It is a profoundly conservative approach and is not – as is often thought – a radical shift.

I have often imagined meeting a native of one of the high mountain valleys of Papua New Guinea where they have never met anyone of European descent and have never heard anything of our ideas. I could imagine telling them of a tribe of white-skinned, blue-eyed people living on an offshore island on the other side of the world.

If I told them that these offshore islanders believe that the universe came into existence by a series of accidents and that although it works in a beautiful and orderly way, it was designed by nobody and for no purpose, they would probably say, 'They must be a very superstitious tribe!' It simply would not fit their plausibility structure. But those assumptions, which I have perhaps caricatured a little, are those that govern the thinking of many of our contemporaries. So faith is primary and doubt secondary. Both are necessary.

In our Western culture we have developed and relied upon the use of 'science' which, of course, means knowledge. Science is only another word for 'knowing' but we have separated science from other kinds of knowing in the belief that science gives us what is called 'objective facts' and that things which cannot qualify in that sense are of necessity purely subjective.

This again is a fashion of thought, and an absurd one, because there can be no knowing of anything without a knowing subject. If there is no subjectivity there is no knowledge. So the idea of purely objective knowledge is an illusion, but a most powerful one.

I was once trying to communicate my faith to a young man who finally told me, 'Well, of course, that's just what you think.' The reply to that must surely be, 'Well, did anyone ever find out anything without thinking?' The idea that there is somehow a kind of knowledge which is not what you think, but something quite independent of your thinking, is absurd – but it is a prime and dominant illusion of Western culture.

There has to be a knowing subject and that subject is, by definition, someone moulded by a particular culture and shaped by his or her own psychological make-up.

Furthermore, knowing is not something that just happens to us. It is something we have to achieve, a skill we have to try to learn and in which we may succeed or fail.

Knowing in this respect is a learned achievement that requires our commitment. It is not like a photographic image but rather it is a skill and indeed an achievement that we have to accomplish.

In addition, we only learn by apprenticeship to a tradition of knowing. First there are the established practices and conventions embodied in language. We learn as small children to speak a language which is an apprenticeship into a tradition, a way of perceiving or grasping reality and no knowing is possible without that. This is supremely true of science. Science is profoundly conservative and traditional. No one is accepted as a scientist competent to undertake independent research without undergoing years of apprenticeship in the traditions of scientific method.

How can we be certain that the things we 'know' are really true? This is the momentous point at which, I think, the famous French philosopher René Descartes (1596–1650) led us astray. Descartes lived in a time of scepticism. He inaugurated the seventeenth–century intellectual revolution that laid down the foundation for what we think of as the 'modern' scientific age.

Descartes was convinced that by following the method that he adopted – the method that has guided science ever since – it would be possible to have more than what he would have called mere belief, but instead to have certainties, certain knowledge. He approached this in three stages. He started first with something he could not doubt, his own existence. Descartes wrote, 'Even if I am doubting, that means that I am thinking, and if I am thinking, I exist. [*Cogito, ergo sum*] I think, therefore, I am. That is certain.'

By various arguments, with the precision and certainty of mathematics, he set out to build upon that certainty a body of certain or indubitable truth. That was the second step. Finally he developed what is known as 'The Critical Principle'. This has been the jewel in the crown of Western culture ever since. It is the principle that all claims to knowledge must be tested by those two criteria and anything which falls short of certainty in that sense is not knowledge, but only belief. And as the great philosopher John Locke asserted, belief 'is a persuasion which falls short of knowledge'.

So when we stand up in church and affirm, 'I believe', what we are really saying, by Locke's definition, is that we do not know. Belief is therefore considered something other than knowledge. Knowledge is something that is absolutely certain on the basis of the method that Descartes laid down. It is this ground upon which our so-called modern scientific world has been built.

But for the same reason that I suggested when I talked about doubt, Descartes' critical method was bound for eventual destruction. The Critical Principle has to be subject to the Critical Principle itself. It is obvious that you can only criticise a statement on the ground of comparing it with something else which you believe. So it is always possible to turn this critical scrutiny round on that basis and criticise it. So it is hardly surprising that in the centuries of philosophy following Descartes there has been a descent into increasing scepticism.

David Hume (1711–76), the Scottish philosopher, demolished most of the principles of Descartes. Immanuel Kant (1724–1804), who was the professor of logic and metaphysics at the University of Königsberg, East Prussia, tried to restore the grounds for certain knowledge, but had to conclude that we cannot know ultimate reality and that it must be beyond our knowledge. But how Kant knew that, one does not know! Finally, the German philosopher Friedrich Nietzsche (1844–1900) saw with terrible clarity that to continue in the direction that European culture had taken would lead inevitably and inexorably to the point where we could no longer speak of truth or falsehood, nor of good or bad. Any claim to know the truth would be an exercise of dominance. The only thing that would be certain is the will, and any claim to truth would have to be regarded as a claim to dominance, to power.

As a result, we have relapsed into what is now called 'post-modernism', a sinking into the kind of belief where people say, 'Well, it may be true for you, but it's not true for me.' It is believed that there is no such thing as objective truth. In the field of science there is still a good deal of confidence in the idea of objective truth, but even in this area it has been increasingly eroded.

We have actually reached the point where – with the so-called deconstruction movement in literary criticism – the idea that any text has any meaning of itself is demolished. The ultimate development of that is in the work of Don Cupitt, who simply states: 'Words are purely culture constructions and do not themselves correspond to any reality.' So when we say, 'I believe in God' we are expressing a kind of subjective feeling, but there is no reality to which those words correspond.

It is true that all truth claims are the result of cultural influence. The English language is just one of many languages of the world and if I make a truth claim, I am using this particular language to express or suggest statements of truth that relate or belong to the culture implicit in that language. Where are we if we probe the relationship between words and those things which are not words? Do the words 'I believe in God' correspond to a reality which is not words? Is it not obvious that the relation between words and those things which are not words cannot be a matter of words? It must be something different. And this is where the profound error of Descartes' thinking becomes clear. Descartes, who has been followed by three centuries of Western thought, conceived the human mind as though it was a disembodied, objective eye looking at the world in a disinterested or impartial way. It was as if the mind was not part of the world at all and was looking at it from outside and therefore able to take an objective view – not a view shaped by any particular personal thoughts, feelings or cultural influences.

That detached, or objective view, is of course absurd. The mind is not a disembodied entity; it is part of us. Any knowing that we have of anything arises out of our bodily engagement in the actual business of the world. There is no other way by which we can come to know anything and we test our beliefs about what is the case by acting upon them.

One can see in the simplest of ways how a child learns to understand the world. If a balloon is brought closer to a baby, then that balloon has apparently become bigger. It takes a long time before a baby can understand the idea of distance and perception and it does this by taking hold of objects and feeling them with its hands. In this way you can see a baby exploring the world. If its eyes do not tell it all the truth then it uses its hands. It is only by being embodied in the actuality of the world that we begin to understand it.

We are part of this world which we seek to know. The vast delusion that we have suffered since the work of Descartes is the idea that we are somehow at one remove from it with a kind of spectator's privilege of looking at the world from outside. This non-committed view does not allow the influence of personal commitments or personal interests. Objective knowledge is supposed to be that kind of knowledge.

That is a God's-eye view of the world and we do not have that privileged position. We are a part of the world and everything in it, and our knowing relates to our actual bodily engagement as we try to understand and cope with its reality.

Let us look a little more deeply into what I have called the 'structure of knowing'. Take a piece of paper with writing on it. The lines are just ink marks on a white sheet. That is all they are, from one point of view. When we learn to read we have at first to pay an awful lot of attention to the actual shapes of these ink marks. We have long since passed the time when we even look at the shape of those letters. We have moved on to attend to the meaning they communicate.

This 'from to' structure is fundamental to all our knowing. If we look at a picture with a magnifying glass we see tiny daubs of paint here and there, but it is only when we stand back that we see it as a coherent whole. We see the picture, not by ignoring the little paint marks, but precisely by an action of our mind that integrates all these little markings into a united whole – the single picture. Similarly, the marks of ink on the page are integrated by our minds into a meaning, and we attend to the meaning from these subsidiary clues, of which we are normally quite unconscious. While we are learning to read we have to attend to the clues and, of course, it is an effort, a struggle, to learn. But once we have learnt these clues there is a tacit unconscious integration of them into a whole structure of meaning that crosses an enormous range of our knowing.

The learning of language is one of the first examples of the way we learn by 'apprenticeship' to a tradition. As we go on, we learn words, concepts, models, pictures, theories and hypotheses which to begin with are often strange to us. Asking the question: 'What does this concept mean?' we have to attend to it in the same way the small child pays attention to forming letters while learning to read.

When we have mastered these things, then they become the subsidiaries from which we attend to the focal meaning. And, in that sense, we 'indwell' the tradition. All of our knowing involves indwelling our bodily senses. I am able to see a group of people only because my retina is stimulated by light in various ways. I am not conscious of the process but it is from this process that I attend to the meaning of what I am looking at.

So we have a threefold structure of knowing. First, there are the subsidiaries from which you attend to the focal meaning, and all our learning then involves us in new efforts to integrate a great number of subsidiaries into that focal meaning. So there are the subsidiaries and then the focal meaning. The third element is what

I call the 'heuristic passion'. As I said, knowing does not happen automatically. We have to struggle and that struggle involves trying to find meaning and coherence in all these different and apparently separate details.

This third element, heuristic passion, is the desire and longing to know. It is something we share with animals. One can observe an animal puzzled by something it has never previously seen and watch it as it struggles to discover what it is. This passionate desire to know and to find out things for oneself is fundamental to our nature and something we undoubtedly share with the animal world.

This means that we have to take seriously the personal factors involved in all knowing. Science proceeds by a whole series of personal efforts which involve intuition, a kind of sense that there is a pattern in these apparently meaningless and random facts. There is an intuition that there is something there which can be seen as a meaningful whole.

There is the imagination which can frame a possible picture, a hypothesis of how things are. There exists the patience that can go on, year after year, trying to solve a difficult problem, sometimes failing right up to the end. Einstein spent the last years of his life trying to establish a credible and workable theory that would unify relativity and quantum physics, and failed.

The heuristic passion and courage of Einstein governed the closing years of his life. And what of courage? This involves the willingness to take risks, as Einstein did, because there is always the risk of failure. All of these profoundly personal factors are involved in the business of knowing, and the strange idea that knowing is something that does not involve these subjective elements, that it is something purely objective, is nonsense.

But if you say that, then how do we know that we are in actual contact with the truth? I have emphasised the subjectivity of our knowing, but what about its objectivity? How can we or do we know that as a result of all this we are actually connecting with reality?

In this respect I think there are at least three topics that deserve our consideration. The first token of reality is a sense of meaning. When a scientist struggles to make sense of a whole lot of apparently random data, and suddenly sees a picture that holds it all together, then the conviction occurs that something true has been discovered. The sense of meaning and beauty, of symmetry and coherence – these are the first tests of objectivity.

The second test, of course, is that the scientist publishes these findings and invites other scientists to consider their worth – their truth. This is relevant to the whole question of Christian mission and evangelism. Any belief that we are not prepared to publish is not a real belief. If we believe something to be true, then we must publish it because its truth is universal.

Thirdly, if something is true, it will lead to further truths. This is crucial. Any real discovery will always lead the researcher, the searcher or the scientist onwards towards further discoveries. Many dedicated people have spent years in search of the solution to some problem which led them nowhere. Think of those long centuries spent by thinkers trying to understand the nature of gravity in relation to perpetual motion, or to produce the philosopher's stone which would turn dross into gold. These attempts over hundreds of years have ended in nothing but failure.

The mark of truth is that it always leads on to further truth. And so that gives us a dynamic picture of knowledge, in contrast to the one that Descartes gave us. He, like most of the philosophers of science following him, conceived truth as something buttoned up and complete. There were no doubts or no uncertainties. It was a kind of static picture of truth, something which could only be possible 'from above'.

But a working scientist will give you a different picture of truth. That person knows that there is yet more to be discovered. The test of the truthfulness of what has been discovered is not that there is nothing else to be learned but precisely that it leads onward into further reaches of reality. This is what I would call an epistemology 'from below'. The word epistemology simply means 'the science of knowing' – how do we know anything? It comes from the Greek word *episteme* – knowing.

There is a kind of epistemology 'from above' where, as a philosopher, one looks down on truth claims and judges whether or not they can be sustained. But there is also an epistemology 'from below' which is the way that the scientists actually work, where they know that they have not arrived at the final truth and are always pressing forward and seeking more. But the test that they have made contact with reality will be that they are led on to further discoveries. It is a dynamic conception of truth, unlike that of Descartes.

And so we arrive at an important new area of consideration. I have previously been writing about knowing in the sense that scientists talk about it: knowing the natural world, the world of things. But there is another kind of knowing, which is the knowing of persons. In many languages there are two different verbs to express this notion. In German the verb *wissen* means to know things and *kennen* means to know people. In French *savoir* means knowing things while *connaître* means knowing people. Unfortunately in English there is only one such word, but there is an acknowledged difference between the kind of knowing where the object is a thing and the knowing of a person.

If it is a thing that cannot answer back then I decide what to do about it. I can put it on the laboratory table and dissect it. I can put it through various tests and decide the questions to be asked. I am in control. That is one kind of knowing. But we also know that there is another kind of knowing, coming to know a person. In one sense, you can dissect a person on the operating table and discover how the body works, but then you lose the chance of getting to know that person!

This other kind of knowing is where the object is a subject. The object of my knowing is himself or herself, a subject. Therefore, I am not in full control. If I am to know that person I must be prepared to be questioned myself. I must put my trust in that person. I must be willing to open up and trust that this person is speaking the truth.

There is no other way to get to know a person. So here we use faith in a second sense. They are not two separate senses.

At the beginning of this chapter I wrote that we do not know anything except by an initial act of faith. That is faith considered in its cognitive aspect, that is to say as a way of knowing. But faith also has an affective or emotional aspect; it is more a way of loving, of relationship with another.

Now these two are not separate, but they are two different dimensions of faith. So the question is: 'How are these two moulds of knowing related to each other?' Obviously they are not separate. We do not get to know a person as a disembodied spirit but rather through the acts of speaking and gesture, the actuality of events in this physical world by which people make themselves known to one another. That point is fundamental.

A machine's correct mechanical functioning and structure depends on the skill of the person who built it just as much as it depends upon the quality of the metals and components that went into its construction. It depends on the physics and chemistry of its parts and the competent mechanical design of the person who made it possible.

But if you come across a machine you have never seen before, you can examine it to your heart's content but you will never discover its purpose unless you are told by the maker or by someone who has learned from the maker, how to use it. In other words, the mechanical structure of the machine provides the conditions under which the machine works, but does not provide its meaning or purpose. This belongs to a different level of logic.

If I may return to the context of knowing persons, neurosurgery, for example, has developed enormously in the past few years and doctors can now examine the brain and understand better, with amazing surgical precision, how its complex electrical circuits and synaptic connections work. But no matter how far the neurosurgeon might go in this anatomical and physiological analysis of brain function, it would not tell that surgeon a single thing about what the subject thought or felt. There is no possible way it could. It is a different logical level. Consequently, there is a hierarchy of logical levels in all our knowing.

The laws of chemistry depend upon the laws of physics but physics can never replace chemistry. The laws of mechanics depend upon the laws of physics and chemistry but mechanics cannot be replaced by physics and chemistry. Biology in this sense depends upon all three theoretical laws because a bird or an animal is also, in one sense, a mechanism. Creatures function because they are chemically composed of hard and soft tissue – muscles and blood and so forth – and these tissues in turn comprise the atomic structure of the animal. But neither physics, chemistry nor mechanics can replace biology. There exists a hierarchy of levels, and each level can never fully explain the true function of the higher one.

It is therefore clear that in viewing humanity there is a level above the physical, chemical, mechanical and biological level. You cannot really explain a human being. You cannot come to know a person in the sense that we normally use this term of 'knowing', simply by knowing the physical, chemical, biological and mechanical working of the body. The attempt to explain things on a logical level lower than the appropriate one is known as reductionism and it could be said that the whole of the past three centuries of the so-called modern or scientific view of the world has been an example of reductionism – of trying to explain reality on logical levels, on lower levels than those that are appropriate.

The relevance of all this will emerge later, but in the meantime let us consider that most famous of conundrums in this whole business of knowing as propounded by Plato, who asked these questions: 'What does it mean to seek truth? Is truth something that we know or something that we do not know? If we know truth, why do we seek it? If we do not know it, how can we recognise it when we find it?'

Plato's answer was to invoke the prevailing doctrine of reincarnation. His answer was that essentially truth was recognised, known and remembered from a person's previous incarnation. Today few people accept Plato's explanation, and yet scientists go on their merry way making 'discoveries' without attempting to answer the conundrum: 'What does it mean to search for truth? What does it mean when people talk of the love of truth?'

As I said earlier, heuristic passion is the third component in all our knowing – the passion to understand and find meaning in apparent meaninglessness. So is it not at least possible that heuristic passion is a response in us to something beyond us which draws out that passion?

Research scientist Michael Polanyi (1891–1976) was an academic with many discoveries to his credit. He struggled with Plato's conundrum and felt himself to be drawn onward. He was propelled forward by an intuitive feeling that there was something further to be found, as if there was some hidden meaning, beauty or coherence, in the things that baffled him both as a research scientist and as a human being. He felt himself as a scientist being drawn forward beyond the point of being a scientist. Heuristic passion is a response to something prior to us, touching one of the central truths of our being.

This brings us in a sense to the limits of philosophy. The Christian faith affirms that the ultimate logical level upon which things are to be understood is neither physical, chemical, biological, nor mechanical, but the *personal*, and that our whole existence can only be understood if we take this personal level into account. If that is true, then everything will depend upon whether the one who is the person whose purpose governs all things has revealed that purpose to us. And that, of course, is what the gospel affirms.

Whereas Muslims, for example, maintain that God has simply dictated the truth for us to take it or leave it, the gospel affirms that God's revelation of himself is an action in which truth and grace go together, where truth and love are one. God's self-revelation of himself is exactly what this argument would suggest – something which draws us to himself. And if that is true, then we have to conclude that this is the secret both of knowing and being.

Our knowing is not separate from our being. If this is true (and that is what the gospel affirms to be true) then there is something that causes the acorn to grow into an oak and not a cabbage, or a foetus to become a human being and not a monster. That something which has drawn forth the whole process of evolution is not, as Darwin thought, the result of chance mutations operating from below, but is the response of the created order to the one who has created it and who calls all creation to its proper fulfilment.

This would mean that the heuristic passion at the heart of our knowing is a response to God's calling upon us. Alone in creation we are conscious of this calling to seek the truth and to seek it in him. So contrary to Descartes, we are not dealing with disembodied ideas.

The truth can only be known through incarnation, through the actual presence of God in history, the presence of the one in the midst of history, who calls upon us with the words: 'Follow me!'

That would mean that the ultimate secret of knowing is in following Jesus. When we accept that calling, we are not then people who pretend to know everything. But we know that we are on the way, that we are 'in via', that we have the clue that will lead us into the fullness of the truth.

Obviously there will be those who reply, 'This is irrational. This is a mere leap of faith. It doesn't have a rational basis.' But it is so easy to point out the illusion which underlies that criticism. If this world is ultimately a thing, if everything in this world, including ourselves, is ultimately to be understood in terms of physics, chemistry, mechanics and biology and in the last analysis this world is a thing, then the way to know would simply be by observation and reason.

But if the ultimate reality by which this world is constituted is personal, the eternal love of the triune God, then the only way by which we can come to know the truth is by a personal response to a personal calling. And that is what we affirm as Christians. The Bible states, 'The fear of the Lord is the beginning of wisdom' (Proverbs 9:10). It does not say, 'The fear of the Lord is the beginning of religious education.' It is the beginning of *all* wisdom and this is the clue by which, in the end, we shall understand all things. It also means we have to remind our contemporaries that there is no spectators' gallery.

When that young man told me, 'Well, of course, that's just what you think,' he was typically representing the illusion that there is available to us some kind of so-called objective standpoint where things are not just what you *think* but somehow stand apart from any thinking. This is an illusion. We are in fact called upon to a personal commitment, to understanding and knowing, and the limits of natural theology are at that point.

It is only because we know that God has revealed himself in the grace of our Lord Jesus Christ in the actual flesh and blood of his incarnation, death and resurrection that we are able to recognise the illusion of Descartes. Consequently, we accept our calling to be among those who follow the word addressed to us by the incarnate Lord, and know that this is the way to the truth.

5 AUTHORITY: SCRIPTURE, TRADITION, REASON, EXPERIENCE

On the whole we regard authority as a bad thing. Our culture developed in revolt against external authority. One of the great themes of the eighteenth-century Age of Reason, from which our modern world was largely born, was that of freedom from external authority and the affirmation that true authority must be internal. Individual freedom of thought, freedom of conscience and self-responsibility in finding out the truth – these were the ideas that prevailed.

But freedom of thought cannot be the last word. This is because there is a real world out there and we have to find out about it and discover whether we are right or wrong in what we think. So these freedoms – freedom of conscience and freedom of thought – though they are the absolutely sacred icons of our culture, cannot have, or be, the last word unless we are to substitute virtual reality for the real thing. And we cannot live unceasingly in virtual reality.

We know this in the most practical of ways. We know that a teacher explaining perhaps a theory in geometry, or a poem, will exercise a certain authority in saying to the children, 'Look, this is true and I want you to understand this.' And the children might, to begin with, simply accept what is taught on the authority of the teacher. But, of course, the teacher will not be satisfied if the only answer they can give for the truth of a theory is that their teacher said so. The competent teacher will not be satisfied until the child has seen for himself or herself that what has been taught is true. So in this way, authority is both external and internal.

The woman at the well of Samaria told the people of her village about her experience of Jesus and they took her word. But it was only when they went and saw for themselves that they declared, 'Now we have heard for ourselves, and we know that this man really is the Saviour of the world' (John 4:42). Again, we see the internal and external sides of authority.

Let us begin by discussing the external side of authority. Take the question: 'What are the external authorities for what we believe as Christians?' I suppose a typical Protestant answer might be: 'The Bible.' A typical Roman Catholic answer would be: 'The Bible and tradition.' And there is a long tradition in Anglican theology which says: 'Bible, tradition, reason.'

Let us look first at the Catholic answer, for there is much to be said for it. In a certain sense one can say that the Bible, or at least the New Testament, is subsequent to the church.

When St Paul was writing the letters which form a great part of our New Testament, there was no Bible, at least no New Testament. There was the Bible as those people knew it (what we call the Old Testament), but the apostles themselves were reporting a tradition.

Paul was very careful to say over and again, 'I am handing on to you what I received.' The Latin words are the words which in English become 'tradition': the handing over of what is received.

In the first sermon of Peter, on the day of Pentecost, there is an outline of the story. In 1 Corinthians 15:1 St Paul writes, 'I delivered to you,' and the word he uses is 'tradition'. What he had received he transmitted to them in the form of 'tradition' – that Christ died, according to the Scriptures, and was buried and rose from the dead and was then seen by so many people. So it was the apostles who created what we call the New Testament. In that sense the tradition is prior to the book. The apostles were not simply original thinkers, putting out their own ideas about theology. They were, on the contrary, passing on something given to them, given in the first instance, by word of mouth.

Paul, with the older apostles, Peter, James, John and Barnabas and so forth, was hearing that tradition. What we call the four Gospels have been formed by bringing together traditions that were treasured in the different churches of the early first century by those who had actually heard the words of Jesus and seen his deeds.

St Luke said in the introduction to his Gospel that he had made it his business to find out what the earliest witnesses had to say about Jesus: the relationship between the book and the community was two-way. In one sense it was the community which created the book, but in another sense it was the story they told which created the community and those two have always been reciprocally related to each other.

Those first apostles were always careful to affirm that what they were saying was the true interpretation of the Scriptures, namely the Old Testament. So that the coming of Jesus and the events of the gospel had made it possible, for the first time, to understand the real meaning of those prophecies and laws. Their true meaning had become manifest in the things concerning Jesus so that the heart of the tradition, which they received and carried forward, was that, according to the Scriptures, those things actually happened.

The final fixing of the canon of the New Testament, the decision about which books should or should not be included, was a church decision. Some books were the subject of long debate and doubt. It was only with great hesitation that the second book of Peter, for instance, was included in the canon. On the other hand, the gospel of Thomas, which claims to have been written by an apostle, was rejected. It was judged not to be a faithful representation of the tradition, and if we read the gospel of Thomas today we can see why that was deemed to be so.

In one sense the fixing of the text of our New Testament was a work of the church. But on the other hand, the very fact that the church in that way fixed the canon meant that the church recognised that it was not free to think whatever it wanted. Its thinking must forever be controlled by those writings which represent, with the greatest faithfulness, the authentic tradition concerning the original message relating to Jesus.

What then does it mean to speak of the Bible as the word of God? Let us begin by recognising that the phrase 'the word of God' is used in three respects in the New Testament. It is used first of Jesus himself, then of the preaching of the apostles and thirdly of the written Scriptures. The fundamental use of the phrase is with reference to Jesus himself: God, who in sundry times and various ways had spoken through the prophets, had now spoken through his Son. He was, as St John said, the 'Word made flesh', the Word present as a human life. And we cannot stress and emphasise that point enough.

In the previous chapter we looked at the effect upon all our thinking of the past three centuries, of the vision of truth propounded and advocated by Descartes. He saw the human mind as though it was a kind of disembodied eye. He took as the model of truth what was called an objective view where no subject was involved. The mind was outside of and apart from the observed. Descartes taught us to take as the ideal of truth a so-called objective truth, in which the subject was not involved.

In complete contrast to that, we have an actual man of history, living in a particular time and place, identified and personified as the Truth. So the truth is known in exact contradiction to Descartes. It is known in the first sense in the actual bodily reality of this man Jesus. He *is* the Word of God. So the Word of God is not a detached or merely an intellectual or mental entity, but ultimately Jesus himself.

But then naturally, and secondly, the preaching of Jesus as Lord is described as 'preaching the Word'. The preaching of the apostles is the Word of God. And here again, it is not a detached or objective truth where no subject is involved. It is precisely the Word in action, the Word being engaged in the actual life of the world. So that is the second sense in which the phrase 'Word of God' is used.

The third sense occurs in the written testimony to God's word as given to us in the Scriptures. The recorded writings of the apostles, the prophets and the books of the Old Testament are now understood as being testimony to this Word made manifest, made incarnate in Jesus Christ. So that all the writings we have in the Bible have been Scripture from the very beginning.

It is not the case, to put it bluntly, that there were certain writings which were canonised and came to be regarded as Scripture. It is rather that all of these writings – which are the record of actual involvement in the name of God with the life of the world – are from the very beginning part of the action of God in the world. There is no pre-scriptural phase, so to speak, of these writings.

So there are these three senses, of which the first is fundamental: Jesus Christ, the Word of God; secondly, the preaching of Christ as Lord is the preaching of the Word; and thirdly, the realisation that the record of the testimony of the prophets and apostles in relation to Jesus is in fact the word of God.

For the first 1,400 years of the life of the church the Bible was essentially a book that was not read but heard. There was no printed Scripture. The Bible was known through the liturgy of the church and was read and expounded in church. It was part of the testimony of the church to Jesus Christ. But when printing was invented it created something new and different. It meant the Bible could now be read outside the church by an individual not involved in the actual worship of the church. It was still, of course, within the world of Christendom. It was still being read in the context of Christian faith, because that was the public faith of Europe. But it was liberated from the direct control of the church. It was a control which in many ways came eventually to obscure some of the essential teachings of the Scriptures. So it was read outside the church, but still within Christendom, and read as Scripture, as Holy Scripture.

Then we come to that great intellectual conversion of Europe, called by those who passed through it the Enlightenment or the Age of Reason, when the Bible began to be read, not as Scripture, but simply as a book – one of the many that were filling up the world. It was read, however, not within the tradition which controlled its creation, but within another tradition.

Perhaps the fundamental change that took place during that eighteenth-century intellectual conversion, which created our modern understanding of the world, was the return to the ancient classical view that eternal truths transcended history. These truths were beyond history and were, so to speak, beyond time. These eternal or universal truths were such that history could only provide illustrations but could never form the basis or be the ground itself. One of the most quoted sayings of the Enlightenment came from the German philosopher, G. E. Lessing (1729–81). He asserted: 'Accidental truths of history can never become the proof of necessary truths of reason.'

Sir Isaac Newton's life spanned the seventeenth and eighteenth century and his cosmology, envisioning the universe as a huge clock mechanism, which operates indefinitely, was perhaps one of the eternal truths of reason: it was timeless, not based upon any historical happening and – if you come to see it that way – just how things were. But, as the Bible is a story of happenings in history, one might find within it illustrations of eternal truths, but they cannot be the source of our knowledge of truth because – remember Descartes – truth is something known only as an objective reality. In other words, the mind contemplates the world from outside.

How was the church to respond to that position? Broadly speaking, there were two possibilities which we have come to call 'liberal' and 'fundamentalist'. I do not like these labels because they are so often used as an excuse for not listening to the other person – but they are helpful.

The liberal response was fundamentally an evangelical missionary reaction: how can we get the people of this modern world to listen to the Bible? How can we make the Bible intelligible to this modern age? This was what the liberal tried to answer. And the father of the whole liberal movement was the great German theologian, Friedrich Schleiermacher (1768–1834). He said that deeper than all the findings of science and metaphysics there was something fundamental in human nature which urged that we were all ultimately dependent upon God. We are not our own sovereigns.

Whatever our beliefs, we know at heart that we are dependent creatures. There is a sense of absolute dependence upon a greater reality. Schleiermacher sought to find a standing ground from which he could convince the rationalists of his time that the Bible had something to say.

Into our Christian thinking this blessed word 'experience' was launched, where religion became a matter of experience and of internal feelings. Until the nineteenth century, the English word 'experience' was used in the sense in which we now say 'experiment'. Its use in our modern sense came from Germany in the nineteenth century and has now become widely accepted. You do not ask: experience of what? It is just experience that came to be valued as the heart of religion and, of course, Christianity. But not uniquely of Christianity because all religions are full of religious experience. And so, the Bible came to be valued as a marvellous treasury of religious experience.

But then if you begin to ask about the truth of the Bible from the point of view of the enlightened modern world, then you begin to ask all those questions raised by what is called the 'historical-critical' method. This method has dominated theological colleges and seminaries for the past hundred years or so. On examination it is found that the historical-critical method is based upon a whole set of assumptions about what is possible. And on the basis of those assumptions – drawn from another source, not from the Bible – you decide how to understand the Bible and how much of it can be accepted.

The positive fruit of this movement is that there arose a serious and determined effort to disentangle the sources which have been brought together in the Bible, as we have it now, and to examine the various oral and written traditions that have been brought together in this book we call the Bible. But, as I have said, the essential heart of this whole response was how the message of the Bible could be made intelligible to the modern world. And it was in that sense a missionary intention.

It is only now that we can see it was the wrong reaction. The question to the world should have been put the other way round: 'How can the world make any sense at all without the gospel?' But perhaps it would have been too difficult, in the wake of the triumphant Age of Reason, to see that this was the real question.

The other response is the one labelled 'fundamentalist', also shaped by the Enlightenment. Indeed, it is impossible to live in this modern world without being moulded and influenced to a great extent by the Enlightenment. The fundamentalist response takes the form that if the Bible is the word of God, then it must have that kind of certitude which Descartes had taught us to regard as the benchmark of truth. And so it must be affirmed that the Bible is verbally inerrant in every statement and that it possesses that kind of objective certainty which Descartes regarded as the only real knowledge. This means we are imposing upon the Scriptures a concept of truth foreign to them.

To use a simple illustration. When St Paul wrote to the Corinthians, 'I thank God that I baptised none of you – oh yes, I baptised Crispus and Gaius, and the household of Stephanus, but I don't remember who else' (1 Corinthians 1:14–16 paraphrased), he was obviously not writing a kind of inerrant text to satisfy Descartes. It was a different kind of language. And to impose upon it a concept of certitude that has arisen from a particular philosophical tradition is to do injustice and even violence to the Scriptures.

If we want to know what the word of God is, we must not begin by first deciding what it is or what it must be, and then imposing that view upon the Scriptures. We have to find out from the Scriptures themselves what the word of God is, how God speaks to us. And the fundamental mistake is to forget the great insight of the Reformation – that our knowledge of God is by grace through faith.

Our knowledge of God is not the kind of thing that Descartes was advocating. It is a knowledge that comes through atonement, reconciliation and forgiveness. It comes through the gracious action of God addressed to us as human beings who need to repent and be converted. It is a different kind of understanding of truth, and that is the fundamental point to which we must cling.

Look at the Anglican triad: Scripture, tradition, reason. One can understand the inclusion of reason because we have to use our reason in reading the Bible as in anything else. But the point is that reason is not an independent source of information about what is the case. Reason is the faculty by which we make sense of the material and data that is given.

All rational discourse has two characteristics. First of all, something has to be taken for granted. There has to be some data, something given. Secondly, rational discourse always operates within a tradition, which in turn implies language. Reason cannot operate without a language and languages are different. Language cannot operate effectively without a variety of symbols, concepts and models. No reasoning can take place without information, a tradition, and language. In this context language goes beyond mere communication, or the signalling of wants or desires – the type of communication available to animals – and enters the realm of categorising and symbolising reality, which in turn enables reasoning to take place.

The Christian use of reason is that exercise which takes as the data, as the given, the fact of the gospel. The gospel takes the incarnation, death and resurrection of Jesus Christ as what is given. We should not try to go behind it, for it is the starting point. It operates within the tradition of Christian belief which has developed from that beginning.

But if reason is invoked in the sense in which I am afraid it has often been, it is really reason based upon the tradition that stems from the Enlightenment. This takes as the fundamental data simply the facts available for empirical observation by the methods of modern science in the modern world. So that one tradition is brought into play as the critique of another. It is not the independent exercise of reason.

One of the most famous philosophical works of the Enlightenment was Immanuel Kant's *Religion Within the Limits of Reason Alone*. For Kant it was reason, as he understood it, which provided the basic tradition, and religion must be acceptable only as it fits into that tradition. Nicholas Wolterstorff, a modern philosopher, has written an excellent little book called *Reason Within the Bounds of Religion* and the writer points out that all reasoning takes place within a tradition of reasoning and that for most of human history it has been religion that has provided the tradition within which reason works.

In the world of Islam the Koran is understood to be the actual verbatim dictation by God in the Arabic language and to be accepted, whether you understand it or not, simply as God's revelation of the truth. And because all translation means interpretation – since you cannot translate something without at least trying to understand it – and since human understanding is always fallible, it is therefore an article of faith in Islam that the Koran cannot be translated.

If you pick up an English version of the Koran you will notice that it is called 'an interpretation of the Koran' never 'a translation'. In order to actually hear God's word you must learn Arabic but even then you are not expected to understand. You may try, but it is not expected. It is a purely external authority and the ideal of Islam is that one should be able to recite the entire Koran in Arabic.

By contrast, we look at Jesus because the parallel is not Koran and Bible, but Koran and Jesus. It is Jesus who is the Word of God in the primary and fundamental sense and Jesus, as we know, did not write a book. The only knowledge we have of his writing is when he wrote in the dust when a woman was charged with adultery. Jesus could have written a book but he did not. He gathered a company of disciples and he called them 'friends'. He told them: 'I do not call you servants because a servant does not understand what his master is doing. I have called you friends, for everything that I have heard from my father, I have made known to you' (John 15:15).

What we find in the Gospels is exactly what I have been trying to describe: an apprenticeship to a tradition. Jesus took his disciples as apprentices and, as we know, apprenticeship means much more than reading a book. One cannot become a doctor simply by reading medical textbooks. There is no alternative to actually becoming an apprentice to a skilled doctor, watching the expert at work and following by example.

And so it was with Jesus. He did not issue a manual of instructions. He entrusted the revelation of God to this company of friends who were not simply slaves, but real friends, who were to understand what he was saying. And that is why we have different accounts of the words and deeds of Jesus in the four Gospels. We do not have any parable or miracle about which we can say we know exactly what Jesus said or did.

From Descartes' point of view we have no reliable certainty. This is the charge the Muslims make against Christians. If you have been in discussion with Muslims you will know that the fact that we have four Gospels, and not one, is used by them as an argument to prove that we have lost the original Gospel, the *Injil*, and that what we have is a series of botched attempts to recover it. But this is not something to regret; it is fundamental to our faith as this is the way God has made known his revelation to us.

There was an attempt in the early Syriac church to overcome this difficulty by combining the four Gospels into a single narrative, the *Diatessaron*, which comes from Greek and means 'through four', but the church rejected the idea. These four distinct Gospels were kept as they are, in true obedience to the intention of Jesus. This helps us to see what it means for God to reveal himself to us. It is precisely through this presence of the living man Jesus Christ, apprenticing a group of friends to learn and to follow, that God has chosen to reveal himself.

Now we come to the great thing which is absolutely central – the work of the Holy Spirit. It is only if we understand the Christian teaching about the Holy Spirit that we have the clue to overcoming this dichotomy between objective and subjective which has almost paralysed the thinking of our modern world.

First, according to the teaching of the apostles, we have the work of the Spirit in communicating the word of God through the mouths of the prophets. It is by the work of the Spirit that they were enabled to communicate the word of God to their times. Then we have the great event of Pentecost which enabled the apostles to communicate the Word of God incarnate in Jesus to their contemporaries. It is by the power of the Spirit that they were enabled truly to interpret Jesus to the world around them.

Next we have the great passage in St John where Jesus, on the eve of his passion, said to his disciples, 'There are many things I have to tell you but you cannot bear them now' (John 16:12). There was a vast amount which that little company of Palestinian Jews in the first century could not know; they could not have a universal knowledge. There was much that they had to learn, but he told them, 'You cannot bear them now, but the Spirit of truth when he comes, he will guide you into the truth as a whole ... for he will take what is mine and show it to you. All that the Father has is mine; therefore I said that he will take what is mine and show it to you' (John 16:12–15).

In one sense there has been a full revelation: 'He who has seen me has seen the Father,' said Jesus (John 14:9b). So, in one sense, it was a full revelation and yet there was a vast amount to be learnt. And in the New Testament itself we see the disciples beginning to learn and, led by the Spirit, to start going beyond what Jesus had said, for example, in the matter of circumcision.

The work of the Spirit cannot be separated from the name of Jesus. As St Paul and St John said, the test that it was truly the Holy Spirit was that it led to the confession of Jesus as Lord. So the Spirit is not something, as it were, that goes beyond Jesus, but the Spirit illuminates the world in the light of the revelation in Jesus Christ.

It often is said that this makes us sectarian. And if people say,

'But the Spirit's work is much wider than this talk about Jesus,' the answer is, 'All that the Father has is mine' – so the name of Jesus is not a sectarian name. Everything that exists belongs to Jesus. And it is the work of the Spirit through the church down the ages – as the church moves into new continents, new generations and new cultures – to illuminate the world in the light of Jesus Christ so that the truth, the truth in all its fullness, is seen to be present in Jesus Christ.

So in this way this objective-subjective divide is healed. There is the objective given reality of Jesus Christ: this man of Nazareth who belonged both to a particular time in history and to a specific human culture. He was not part of Chinese or African culture and nor was he part of the twentieth century. His life was an objective fact and we may study him as we listen to the Scriptures, and seek to understand them. There is at the same time this working of the Holy Spirit in our hearts which enables Jesus to illuminate the whole of our experience as we move onwards through the history of the world and across all nations and cultures.

I find the Eastern Orthodox way of putting this most helpful, because they say that the Word and the Spirit are the two hands of the Father. The Word (Jesus in the flesh) and the Spirit (universal, everywhere, present in all ages and times) are the two hands of the one Father. They are not two different things. And this is one more place where the doctrine of the Trinity is not a puzzle, but the solution to a puzzle, because there is no other ultimate solution to this dichotomy between subjective and objective.

How in practice do we read the Bible? I think we can waste a lot of time talking about our doctrine of Scripture when what is important is the practice of how we actually treat the Scriptures. We first need to recognise that as we read the Scriptures we are apprentices to a tradition and have much to learn.

It is not that we should simply take it as a Muslim takes the Koran, whether we understand it or not. We should open our hearts and minds to what is given and seek in our total daily life to grasp more fully what it means. The external authority is there but our task is to internalise it and understand it and not to pretend that we understand all of it – or even that we can accept it all. Our business is to allow it to shape our thinking and practice so that we see ourselves as apprentices in this great tradition, of which the Bible is the central clue.

All of this must be tackled in the context of actual discipleship because there can be no apprenticeship which involves the mere reading of a book. It must be worked at against a background of worship, obedience and discipleship. One result of the Enlightenment is that the Bible has been taken out of the church and perhaps lodged too much in the universities and schools for academic study. Of course, it is perfectly legitimate to study the Bible in academic institutions. The universities may help us with all kinds of insights, and thank God for that. But the real understanding of the Bible can only be in church, in the context of worship and obedience and in connection with the tradition of all the saints who sought to be faithful, in their own day, to the teaching of the Bible.

We have to use our reason in reading the Bible. But it is a reason which is based not upon some other tradition but on the tradition of the Bible itself. Obviously, when we read the Bible there are great tensions. Put the book of Joshua alongside the Sermon on the Mount and you have a mind-blowing contradiction. In many other places, there are further tensions. Take, for example, the passages on justification by faith written by St Paul and those written by St James. Consider the nature of the state in Revelation 13 and in Romans 13: in Romans, the Roman Empire is the power ordained by God while in Revelation it is the beast out of the Abyss.

How do we cope with them? How do we deal with these tensions? The ultimate clue is in Jesus himself. We must recognise that in the Bible God is leading a people to a deeper understanding of his nature and that we therefore have to read the Bible in this light. When Jesus begins a statement with the words, 'You have been told in old times, but I say unto you', this is not an absolute discontinuity. Jesus is instead bringing an old commandment to its full strength and deeper understanding in his own teaching.

We have to recognise that in the Bible we have the story of God leading a people into an ever deepening understanding. That means that we have to read every text in the context of the gospel itself, for it is the clue to our understanding of Scripture.

It means that we read every text in its cultural context. Let me give another simple illustration. It is said that St Paul accepted slavery and therefore we cannot trust him. But slavery was an integral part of his culture and you cannot simply jump out of your society or your time. The Bible forbids usury – the taking of interest on loans. In modern usage usury means the charging of iniquitous rates of interest, but the charging of reasonable rates is nevertheless integral to our own present economic system. We know that the Bible forbids it yet we all practise it. We cannot leap out of our society. Paul could not suddenly propel himself out of the first-century society in which he lived, but he was able to plant the seeds of change. When Paul considered the case of the runaway slave Onesimus he did not tell him to go underground and become a fugitive. Instead, he sent him back to his master, but with a new status. This was the status of a representative of the apostles in the house of Philemon.

Paul thus introduced into that existing institution of slavery something which would eventually transform it. This simple illustration is true in many other cases. We must always read any text in the context of the culture of its time. So in reading the Scriptures we should try to understand their direction, and the meaning to which the texts point, in relation to their place and time.

But the ultimate tension in the Bible, which causes us discomfort, is that straining between the holy wrath of God and the holy love of God – a tension which lies at the very heart of the being of God. And that is a tension which within this life we will never fully overcome. We have to take with the greatest seriousness both those passages of Scripture which speak of the holy wrath of God, his rejection of sin in every form, and those passages which speak of the all-inclusive and utterly forgiving love of God for the sinner. In our human strength we cannot hold that tension but it is in the atoning work of Jesus Christ, in that cross which is both the judgment and the salvation of the world, that the clue lies by which we can grasp these tremendous tensions within the Scriptures.

We must allow the Scriptures to shape our minds and teach us how God speaks to us, what it means to speak of the Word of God. We must allow the Scriptures to play such a vast part in our lives that we think in terms of the horizon that Scripture gives us. It is in the light of the Scriptures as a whole that we eventually come to understand our own lives. We come to understand who we really are, rather than avoiding who we are. We realise where we have come from and where we are going, and what choices are available to us on the way. It is only when we discover how to live in this manner that we learn what it really means to speak of Scripture as being the word of God.

6 CREATION: THINGS VISIBLE AND INVISIBLE

'In the beginning God created the heavens and the earth' (Genesis 1:1). This was the absolute beginning. Before that, there was neither space nor time, nothing at all. It was the complete and total origin of all things: 'In the beginning, God.'

In Colossians 1:16 St Paul makes this more explicit: '… all things were created: things in heaven and on earth, visible and invisible'. That is an important clarification of what is intended by the words 'heaven' and 'earth' – both the visible and invisible. If we had kept that firmly and consistently in mind I think perhaps some of the futile arguments that have gone on in the past among theologians might have been avoided.

For example, there have been prolonged arguments and disputes about whether something was right because God commanded it, or whether God commanded it because it was right. To advance that idea implies that there is something called 'right' which existed, as it were, before God or exists apart from God. The thinking that is intrinsic to the phrase 'all things invisible' protects us from this notion. We think of concepts such as right and wrong, beauty or coherence, as though they possess a kind of timeless existence, but this is not so. All things visible and invisible in heaven and on earth have their sole origin in God's mighty word.

If we could only adopt the attitude enshrined in that famous little notice that Harry S. Truman placed on his desk in 1945 when he was President of the United States: 'The buck stops here.' He assumed responsibility for things he would not pass on to someone else. In a sense, in all our intellectual inquiries, we need to have that little motto in front of us. Here is where the final questioning stops and we have to humbly accept the answer.

I want to discuss five points that flow from those first chapters of Genesis about God's creation. The first is that there is an emphasis on distinguishing and separating things one from another: light from darkness, sea from land, the different species of animals and plants, the distinctness and specificity of everything that has been created.

The second point is the fact that the created world has been given a sort of autonomy. It has a life of its own. Plants, animals and humans are able to reproduce their own species. The created world has a being, a life and a movement of its own. This creation is not just a kind of extension of God or an emanation from him, but distinct from him. It was so clear-cut and well-defined that on the seventh day God could rest. The creation went on. God did not have to keep pushing it along all the time. He could rest and contemplate his creation and, as we shall see, that is a very important point for practical discipleship.

The third aspect is that the whole world was brought into existence as a home for the human family. The purpose and meaning of it all was that it should be such a home. I think perhaps this emerges most strikingly in what is said about the creation on the fourth day: the creation of the sun, moon and stars. These words were almost certainly written during the time when the people of Israel were enslaved under the mighty Babylonian Empire, working in powerless bondage under the shadows of those enormous temples and palaces that we know existed in Babylon.

For the Babylonians – like so many other cultures in the world – the sun, moon and stars were gods. They were supernatural heavenly bodies, divine entities to be worshipped and prayed to. But here our text says this was not so. They were lamps placed in the sky for the home that God had made for his family. The whole meaning of the creation was that it was to be a home for God's family.

The fourth thing to be grasped is that the human family has been given a particular responsibility, and that is to cherish the creation. It has been given a delegated responsibility from the Creator to bring the creation into the perfection which the Creator desires. And this in itself is an important message in relation to all our ecological fears of the present time. It was not God's intention that the world should become a wilderness. It was to be a garden for the human family to nourish and cultivate.

Humankind was granted responsibility for the naming and classifying of animals so that there was from the onset a relationship with them. The Christian scholar C. S. Lewis suggested in one of his books that it was part of our responsibility as human beings to do all we could to bring animals to the fullness of their potential. Take, for example, a faithful dog. One thinks of those marvellous animals used by shepherds on the Cheviot Hills in northern England. Such dogs are incredibly intelligent and responsive, and if you contrast them with a wild creature like a fox or a wolf, you then begin to realise what God intended human beings to do in relation to the potential of animal existence. We are given a delegated responsibility to bring the whole created world into that perfection for which God made it.

My fifth point is that God looked each day at everything he had made and saw that it was good. This is a wonderful phrase, and it is repeated after each day of creation until it culminates, on the sixth day, with God's affirmation that all he has made is 'very good' (Genesis 1:31). This phrase contrasts sharply with so much of human religion which has often regarded the world as a bad and dangerous place, a place of darkness. The Christian reformer John Calvin, in a wonderful description, considered the world to be 'a theatre for God's glory' – a place where his glory was reflected in the created world.

If we compare this with pagan views of the created world, we see how great the difference is. I am, of course, using language rather loosely here because 'pagan' is a word of broad meaning. It includes an immense variety of different beliefs, but there are certain common things, which are fairly widespread in the world, which pagan views share. For example, there is the idea that nature itself is in some way divine and that it is the ultimate reality. This is expressed in primitive animistic forms where trees and rivers and mountain tops are seen as places where divine energies rest. It can also be seen very clearly in many forms of Hinduism where the powers of nature are identified with God.

If, for example, you go to a Sivaite temple you will see in the central shrine a phallus, a symbol of the potency of human sexuality, and guarding the door a bull, the supreme symbol of pure animal power. Those sheer powers of nature are seen as divine and as the ultimate reality.

Alternatively, and these two things can go together, nature is seen to be transient. All natural things die and pass away – except things like mountains – but even these eventually erode. Most of nature is marked by transience. The plants blossom, grow, and then fade and die, as do human beings and animals. So throughout human history there has been a strong tendency to feel that ultimate reality is beyond nature, that it must be something transhistorical, eternal. It is something to be grasped by the mind, rather than these fleeting things that we know by our rather inadequate senses of sight, feeling and hearing.

This was clear in the classical world into which the Christian church was first launched. According to Plato, the ultimate realities were ideas and non-material things. All the different things in this world were shadowy or imperfect representations of a perfect reality that existed in an invisible world of ideas. Or, according to Aristotle, a sharp distinction existed between 'substance' and what he referred to as 'accidents'. What we see, hear, touch and feel are the accidents of things. But the real substance, what lies behind those accidents, is something we can never know.

There was a sharp distinction between what the Greeks called the sensible world and the intelligible world. The sensible world was grasped by the five senses of sight, smell, hearing, taste and touch. On the other hand, the intelligible world is that which we apprehend or perceive with the mind, or perhaps contemplate with the spirit. So the way to ultimate reality was to bypass the material things of the visible world, and to bypass those accidental happenings in history which cannot give us ultimate truth, and to press on beyond them. To pass through this visible world to an eternal invisible world beyond would be achieved by the powers of human reason or mystical contemplation, self-transcendence and all the various techniques of yoga.

By implication history could not have any real significance. History might appear to be linear and moving onwards, but this was an illusion. It was really just going round in circles and everything that had happened would happen again. Our understanding of history would therefore be modelled on our perception of nature as a perpetual cycle of growth, development, maturity, decay and death, followed by new growth – and so on. So the actual happenings of history could have no ultimate significance.

Those were the dominant ideas of the pagan world into which the Christian gospel was projected. During the period when Christianity was a persecuted minority religion struggling for its life and winning its way by the testimony of its martyrs, there could be no mature discussion between those who stood for the Christian gospel and those who held these pagan views. But once Christianity was acknowledged as a permitted religion, and eventually as the religion of the Empire, the way was opened for vigorous discussion. This occurred especially in the great intellectual centre of Alexandria, the greatest in the world at that time, with its tremendous library. And in the fourth and fifth centuries many vigorous intellectual discussions took place between Christian thinkers and the practitioners of science and philosophy.

Those early Christian theologians learned from these discussions that nothing could be built on classical philosophy. The gospel provided a completely new starting point. If the Logos, the divine reason for the existence of all things – by which they were made and for which they existed – had actually appeared in human history in the person of Jesus Christ, then that had to be the starting point of all our thinking. From that standpoint it was then possible to step back from the dominant classical worldview and pose some specific questions from which certain principles emerged which ever since have defined and determined the development of European thought.

The first principle is that since the world is the creation of a rational God, and since God has created us in his image, then a rationality prevails which is within the grasp of reason. We can therefore take it as a matter of faith that in principle the universe is ultimately comprehensible, though there may be many things that we do not yet understand. And that is the indispensable foundation upon which modern science has been built.

If the universe was a place where all kinds of demons and spirits could perform their arbitrary deeds according to whim and fancy, then there could be no certainty of the existence of a rational universe. Why do European scientists take it for granted – unlike the thinking in many other parts of the world – that if two similar experiments are conducted in two different places with dissimilar results, then there must be a mistake? The passionate conviction that these things cannot be totally irreconcilable, that one must be able to find some pattern of thought which will enable us, coherently, to hold these things together, is what has made possible the enormous advance of science.

This has one particular illustration with regard to the so-called 'heavenly bodies'. In pagan thought, most certainly in the thought of Aristotle which dominated the science of the first centuries, the sun, moon and stars were heavenly bodies. They were not made of the same four elements of earth, air, fire and water of which this world was made, but were of a different kind of being. The Christian theologians declared, 'No. Since God created them all, they are all of the same kind.' One of the ironies of the history of thought is that when the controversial physicist and astronomer Galilei Galileo (1564–1642) got to work with his telescope and concluded that the moon was made of the same stuff as earth, he was roundly condemned by the church because the church, earlier in the twelfth century, had taken Aristotle on board again. That is one of the many ironies in the history of the relation between science and religion.

Since creation is not an emanation, this created world has a relative autonomy but it is not an absolute autonomy. The world has a measure of independence which does not depend for its continuing existence on God constantly causing all things to happen. In the thought of Aristotle – and here he is followed by Islam to this day – everything that moved was governed by God. The stars move because God is moving them. The concept of momentum was wholly foreign to classical thought.

If I throw a ball into the air, we now take it for granted that in the absence of gravity it will go on moving with its own momentum gained from that initial thrust. But that was a concept unknown to the classical world. If the ball went on moving, it was because God was pushing it along. It was the rediscovery of the concept of momentum in the Middle Ages that made possible the revolutionary physics and mathematics of Sir Isaac Newton. This is one example of the way those early theologians challenged the prevailing worldview and insisted that this world, since it was a creation, had a relative independence. Everything that happened was not the direct action of God.

But the great and difficult question to which we must return is this: 'How much autonomy does the world have?' It is possible to go to one extreme and suggest that it has almost complete autonomy. This is the image of the world as a clock which functions perfectly without the clock-maker's interference. If the clock-maker was highly skilled, having made the clock and wound it up, there would be no need for further interference.

That way of looking at the world, which is called deism, the belief in a creator who did not intervene in the universe, was a dominant view in the seventeenth century when Newton was working.

Although Newton's theology was deist, he nevertheless believed that the 'clock' needed occasional adjustment and that God would do this if and when it became necessary.

But it was not long before the clock-maker was made redundant. With the approach of the nineteenth century the view emerged where the dominant picture of the world was seen as a pure mechanism which worked without reference to any divine purpose and from which anything that we might call the supernatural, had been banished.

There is a well-known story of the famous physicist and astronomer Pierre-Simon Laplace (1749–1827) who produced a great work on astronomy that contradicted Newton's worry that perturbations in planetary orbits would lead to long-term instability of the solar system. He presented it to Napoleon, who after reading it, said, 'But, Monsieur Laplace, I do not see any reference to God in this work.' To which Laplace replied, 'I have no need of that hypothesis.' (Newton thought that divine intervention was necessary to ensure stability.) The reply of Laplace could be a motto for nineteenth century science which still has such a large influence in our own time. It depicts a world so totally independent that the very idea of God becomes unnecessary.

The other extreme, pantheism, perceives the world as being completely dependent on God at all times. God is in everything and doing everything, permanently pervading the universe so that you cannot, as it were, distinguish God from the world. God is immanent and cannot be distinguished from the world.

The post-Renaissance Dutch Jewish philosopher Baruch Spinoza (1632–77) coined the widely used phrase *Deus sive Natura* – 'God, though equally it is Nature.' God was identified with nature because he impregnated and saturated the whole world. That way of thinking had reasserted itself around the time of the Renaissance because of the growing influence of Platonism.

So the Christian theologian has always had to find a way between those two extremes: deism, which makes the world so independent of God that there is no need for God, and pantheism, where

God disappears into the world. Contemporary examples of this pantheistic way of thinking are the New Age movement and the so-called 'creation spirituality' espoused by Dr Matthew Fox and the University of Creation Spirituality in California, USA.

Because of the incarnation, it is permissible to speak in terms of material means for our salvation. Let me explain what I mean. The Greeks developed the science and practice of medicine to a considerable degree, but the Hebrews rejected it. In the Old Testament there was no place for doctors. Healing was the direct work of God, the answer to prayer; it was part of forgiveness and because of this there was no place for medicine.

But the early Christian theologians argued that because God had used in the incarnation the actual material life of Jesus Christ to bring about the salvation of the world, consequently the use of material things for God's purposes of healing and salvation could not be rejected. So in contrast to the Hebrews the Christians accepted and took advantage of Greek techniques and achievements in medicine. From this they developed the whole ethos of the healing ministry which since then has always been such an integral part of the church's work.

On that basis, of course, much greater and wider developments occurred. What we now call technology emerged, as well as all the different ways that material things have been developed to further human welfare. The great apostle of this movement was Francis Bacon, the Renaissance philosopher, who passionately believed that it was essential to develop science in order to improve and elevate the human race. In that respect we know how much has been accomplished, but we also know, sadly, how technology can become a terrible instrument in the cause of evil.

How is this question of autonomy to be answered? We have seen the two extremes. On the one hand deism teaches that the world carries on by itself without interference. On the other hand pantheism sees the world pervaded by God and that everything that happens in it is his work. How do we navigate the correct course between them? How is the created world related to God? That is perhaps one of the most difficult and inescapable problems in all Christian thinking about the world. At one end of the scale, and it comes in different forms, you could say there is no relationship. Or to put it the other way, the world has no independence at all. As I have said, Islam, following the Aristotelian tradition, is a religion whose adherents believe that everything that happens in the world is the direct action of God. The movement of a star or even a single stone is the direct action of God. And in that Islam follows the Aristotelian doctrine of the 'prime mover'. Perhaps one of the most disturbing things to have happened in the course of Christian history was St Thomas Aquinas' attempt to synthesise biblical faith and this Aristotelian–Islamic rationalism. In this he came dangerously close to equating the God of the Bible with Allah – the prime mover of Aristotle and Islam – and I think even today we are still troubled by this confusion.

The reason why Islam rejects the central Christian doctrine of the crucifixion – that the Son of God died on the cross for our salvation – as simply impossible is because the Muslim world believes that Jesus was an apostle of God, and that God could not, and would not, have killed his own apostle. And since everything that happens in the world is the direct action of God, it would be incredible, impossible, indeed blasphemous, to hold the belief that Jesus died on the cross.

But the other extreme is to claim total autonomy for the world, to see it as a closed system controlled entirely by cause and effect. In the often repeated assertion of nineteenth-century positivism, all causes were adequate to the effects they produced and all effects could be explained by the causes which produced them. Here there is no place for the supernatural. The way the world functions and is to be understood is entirely in terms of its own internal rules of action, or laws.

We can neither ask God to interfere in a world which is independent of him, nor on the other hand if the world is completely dependent on him can we ask God to change his mind to suit our wishes. In both cases prayer, intercession, miracles or divine providence – the belief that God rules over all things for the good of those who love him – become impossible.

I do not think that there is what could be called a metaphysical solution to this problem. I think it has to be, as in everything else, a solution that depends on faith in God's grace as revealed to us in the Bible.

There is first an orderliness, a pattern, a regularity which God has built into the created world. Genesis speaks of the regularity of the seasons, of day and night, summer and winter, spring time and harvest. God does not act arbitrarily and unpredictably. This orderliness has been made clear in the unravelling by science of the laws and regularities of nature, without which human freedom would be impossible.

We can only act responsibly if we know that the world is not an arbitrary place. If we do not know whether water will boil or freeze under heat then we could not make a cup of tea. All human freedom of thought and action depends upon the regularity God has given to the natural world. It relies upon the fact that God is consistent and not arbitrary or whimsical, that the world is not under the control of capricious little demons and imps who can play havoc with things. This given regularity of the world is the condition upon which our freedom is based.

Next there is human responsibility, and therefore the freedom to obey God. The Old Testament makes it absolutely clear that people are responsible before God. They can sin and repent. God makes them responsible for their actions, so that everything that happens is without doubt not the direct will of God. He has created a world where people possess the freedom to disobey him and act against his will.

Then – and this is a different kind of argument altogether – in our understanding of the regularities of the world, we have to recognise a hierarchy of logical levels. As we saw in Chapter 4, the simplest example would be to take a machine. You can understand a machine on one level in terms of its physical components and mechanical structure. You could understand completely the relationship between cause and effect which makes that machine work, but that does not begin to tell you its purpose – what the machine is *for*. Either the designer of the machine, or someone who has learned from its designer, must tell you. The question of the purpose of the machine is on a different logical level.

There is a whole hierarchy of levels: atomic, molecular, mechanical, biological and so forth. Biology cannot be replaced by physics or mechanics. Chemistry cannot be replaced by physics and so on. And in particular, when we think about human behaviour, we know that from one point of view, at one logical level, it can be fully explained by the mechanical structure of the skeleton and the nerve impulses that move muscles and by the electrical activity in the brain which can be studied by a neurologist.

But none of this explains human motivation or purpose. This again is on a different logical level. We can therefore accept that while in one sense the world can be explained as a self-operating mechanism, it is not the total explanation. To attempt to understand the world, divorced from the purpose of the one who created it, is a logical mistake. It is to misunderstand the difference between logical levels. But it still remains a mystery why God has given us this freedom of choice to disobey him and has given to the world this regularity we cannot ignore or reject, and yet God, in the words of St Paul, 'works for the good of those who love him ...' (Romans 8:28).

It is only by grace through faith that we can understand that. This awareness and insight begins with the cross and resurrection of Jesus. The cross of Jesus is, from one point of view, the most complete contradiction of God's purpose and yet has become, through his workings, the most complete expression in action of his purpose. The cross and resurrection of Jesus are the place where, by faith and in response to grace, we can believe. We can believe even if we cannot completely explain that despite the relative independence God has given the world, he nevertheless overrules all things for the good of those who love him.

Remember Plato's famous conundrum: 'What does it mean to

seek the truth? If we know what truth is, why do we seek it? If we do not know what it is, how will we recognise it when we find it?' Plato's answer was in terms of the doctrine of reincarnation, that when we recognise truth it is because we have remembered something from a previous birth. Few people today accept that.

How do we understand? How can we answer Plato's conundrum? The answer surely involves heuristic passion to which I referred in Chapter 4. This passion to know leaves us unwilling to accept mere confusion. It drives us to seek pattern, order, beauty and coherence in the multitude of things that face us. This could be a jumble of patterns on a page or the total perplexity of our very lives. It is not something which simply arises from below but is the response to the grace of God who, as St Paul says, 'has made us so that we might feel after him and find him'.

If all this is true then it brings all our knowing and being together, because we would then have to understand that it is the same grace of God calling all creation to its full potential, to completeness and perfection. It also explains the specific ways of nature where an acorn grows by these natural and consistent laws into an oak tree and not into a cabbage. It explains the evolution of living creatures in the world as the response of creation to the calling of its Creator and not, as Darwin theorised, by blind forces from below. As human beings we possess an innate ability to make that response conscious. So with all our thoughts and feelings we are able to struggle to try to grasp the meaning of this wonderful and often perplexing world in which God has placed us. If that is the correct way of comprehending then we can understand the Fall because we know that the human story is not simply that of our faithful search for the truth and of our growth towards God's purpose.

If this picture is true then we can understand the Fall exactly as it is portrayed in Genesis 3: as the struggle to know perverted into a desire for personal power. The temptation of the serpent was not to trust God's word but to find out for oneself, so that we would be like God and we would know, not by faith but by knowledge. We would know as God knows. We would no longer innocently believe or trust but would actually *know* good and evil. The turning inwards of the longing for truth, into the self, is the essence of the Fall, and that is why our marvellous achievements in technology in using the powers of nature to serve humanity, have become for us a double-edged sword, for technology may also be used as a terrible instrument of evil.

Finally, as well as the visible world, we must remember that God made all things visible and invisible. Consider again Paul's words in Colossians 1:15–20. Look particularly at the words: 'For by him all things were created: things in heaven and on earth, visible and invisible …' which we repeat in the creed. Paul then spells it out by talking of dominions or principalities. He is talking of power and authority, invisible things, which are nevertheless real and powerful. What does he mean?

We know from the rest of his letters what Paul was talking about because he makes use of this language in many places. Sometimes this language refers to the imperial power, the ultimate political power represented by Caesar in Romans 13. Sometimes it is the Jewish Law in Galatians. Elsewhere it is Greek philosophy in Colossians 2. Sometimes it is the whole establishment that put Jesus on the cross. In 1 Corinthians 2:8 he declares that if the principalities and powers had recognised Jesus they would never have crucified him. And those principalities and powers were represented by the Jewish priests, the scribes, the Pharisees, Pontius Pilate and the mob-like crowd bellowing and shouting for his death.

In every case those powers were represented by something visible. Caesar was a visible human being, but he was not just that; he was the present embodiment of a power that was there long before he was born and would be there long after he was dead.

There exist powers, ideologies, spiritual realities which are represented temporarily in human beings and their institutions but which also have a strange or curious existence of their own. This separate existence is enormously strong. I have become keenly aware of this from talking to such people as industrialists and bankers. From a human point of view these people seem to hold tremendous power but when you talk to them on a personal level they confess that they feel powerless. They feel trapped and helpless in the grip of a vast system which has a life of its own, operating and organising things from which they cannot free themselves. Nationalism, especially when represented in extreme forms, such as Nazism, is a particular example of these intangible forces.

Paul said that such powers were also created by God in Christ for a good and valid purpose because positive intentions and aspirations were found in such things as political authority and economic order. But unfortunately they have become fallen powers, part of this fallen creation. They have sought to absolutise themselves, to confer upon themselves powers which belong only to God. They thus become agents of evil against which we must fight.

But as the New Testament constantly reminds us, in his dying on the cross, Jesus disarmed and dethroned those powers. 'Now is the time for judgment on this world; now the prince of this world will be driven out' (John 12:31). They were not destroyed; they were disarmed. Paul stated in 1 Corinthians (15:24–25) that Jesus must reign until all the powers of the enemy were brought under his feet, and then he would hand the kingdom to the Father.

We live in times when these powers, which still exist and threaten us, have nevertheless been robbed of their final authority. We can therefore do as Paul says: 'Put on the full armour of God ... For our struggle is not against flesh and blood, but against the rulers, against the authorities, against the spiritual forces...' (Ephesians 6:11–12). Our fight is not against other human beings, but against these principalities and powers, these invisible realities which are nevertheless part of the created world, God's creation, a fallen creation, but ultimately redeemed and under the power of Christ.

And so we live by grace through faith in the confidence that God, who in the beginning created all things visible and invisible, will in the end reign in glory over all things and that the earth will indeed be 'the theatre of his glory'.

7 SALVATION: FALL, SIN, REDEMPTION, ATONEMENT, JUSTIFICATION

'God saw all that he had made, and it was very good' (Genesis 1:31).

Thank God for that basic truth at the very beginning of our Bible. But regrettably, we also know that it is not the last word. There follows the story of what we call the Fall. As Christians we understand our world as a good creation which has 'fallen', and the human race as made in God's image and therefore 'good', but 'fallen' and in 'rebellion'. It is at this point that we are very strongly criticised by our culture.

To call someone a sinner is the greatest sin one can commit, as Gandhi once suggested when he remarked, 'To call people sinners is to undermine their humanity.' Many of our contemporaries would say that people need to be encouraged and told that they have great dignity and worth, and to label them sinners is a deep offence against their humanity.

Certainly from the time of the Renaissance onwards, European culture has tried to take an optimistic view of human nature. At the beginning of the 1776 American Declaration of Independence there occurs that momentous 'self-evident' statement that all people are created equal with equal rights to life, liberty and the pursuit of happiness. This was truly a great statement. And happiness was the glorious new buzzword of the eighteenth century.

In the Middle Ages people did not expect happiness on earth, only the first taste of it. They expected happiness to come at the end. But especially from the Renaissance onwards that idea of happiness coming only at the end was regarded as a form of sedition, a sort of treason against humanity. Human nature was good. Of course there were bad people, but basically human nature was good and the task was to tell people so and encourage them to believe it.

We all know about sin. We know it especially because we are able to recognise other people as being sinners. We pass judgment on others and we have a strong tendency to identify sin with particular groups. For example, in the 1945 celebrations on VE Day we were reminded of the appalling evil of Nazi Germany before and during the Second World War. People thought then that this demonic evil must not, could not, and would not ever recur. But we know that evil of this nature is still going on in many parts of the world. It has happened in Bosnia and continues to occur just about everywhere else. There is no doubt at all that the Bible speaks of us as sinners, although as a matter of fact there are very few references to the Fall in the Old Testament, except at the beginning of Genesis.

What grounds do we have for talking of sin? It is there in Genesis 3, but ultimately all Christian doctrine has to be validated at the centre point of the gospel. This is the point of the incarnation, death, resurrection and the victorious Ascension of Jesus Christ. To put it candidly and rather bluntly, we know we are sinners because of what happened on Good Friday. That is the ultimate ground for our affirming that as a whole we are all sinners.

To use an illustration, I once had an experience that was meaningful to me: I used to travel back and forth by ship from England to India and sometimes the voyage would take three or even four weeks. I especially remember one voyage during the second world war when there were enemy submarines about. Those on board all knew that there might come the terrifying cry of 'submarines!' Whenever we went on that ship we all had to carry our lifejackets at all times.

On a long voyage, a ship's company becomes and inhabits a little world of its own. Small groups, cliques and coteries form in the usual way and there are nice people and those who are not so nice. People naturally make distinctions between one another. We made friends with some while inevitably there were others we did not want to know. But we all knew that if the cry 'Submarines!', went up then all of that superficial social grouping would instantly disappear. Only one central issue would remain: Life or Death. In that we were all together, literally in the same boat, whatever we thought of one another. And in life itself it is the same, we are all in this together in the same situation.

That illustration, of life together aboard ship in those circumstances, is a way of expressing what the cross means. Because what happened on Good Friday was this: when Almighty God personally met us, the human race face to face, it was, for practical purposes, the unanimous decision of that representative company of the human race that he must be destroyed.

The crucifixion of Jesus was not the deed of a few bad people. It was, on the contrary, the work of those who were, and are, accounted the 'best' people: the righteous, the priests, scribes, governing officials and, of course, the crowd in the streets. So unless we take the view that we are a very special case, we must consequently conclude that essentially what happened was that the human race came face to face with its Creator and its response was to seek to destroy him.

That utterly crucial and central moment in universal history is the ground on which we are compelled to say that all of us, the good and bad together, are sinners. If that was the last word, then there could be no future for the human race. The only authentic response to what happened would be what Judas did when he went out and hanged himself. What future is there for humanity if that is what we are? But, of course, it is not the last word, because the crucifixion of Jesus, while on the one hand the act of sinful men and women, on the other hand was the work of Christ himself who went deliberately to that meeting point to give himself up for the life of the world.

It is at that point where we are judged and condemned without distinction. The cross cannot be used as a banner for one part of humanity against another. It is the place where we are all, without distinction, unmasked as the enemies of God. But it is also the place where to all, without distinction, there is offered the unlimited kindness and love of God.

While in a sense the first reaction to the cross is that it is a death sentence upon all of us, it is nevertheless at the same time the gift of life. So that Paul says, 'I have been crucified with Christ and I no longer live, but Christ lives in me' (Galatians 2:20). This life that I now have is not an extension, a kind of period of prolongation, given to that old self that put Jesus on the cross. It is on the contrary the gift of a new life because he who is the Creator of all life has died in order that I might live. Therefore, Paul has this to say: 'I am crucified with Christ, I am finished. I belong to a world which has no further entitlement to exist, and yet I live. But I live not because *I* live but because he died that I might live, so that the life that I now live is not mine but his, or rather it is a life that I live by faith in the Son of God who loved me and gave himself for me.'

We can only know that we are sinners because we have been forgiven. That seems to me to be absolutely fundamental. We teach the doctrine of original sin because we have been forgiven. Apart from that, the doctrine would simply be unbelievable and impossible, because it is sin itself which blinds us to sin. It is only the forgiven who can truly repent because sin blinds our eyes to the reality of who we are.

So the first and fundamental thing to be said is that we must speak of sin as something that affects and involves all humanity. This is not because we are in a position to pass judgment on anybody else, or because we have looked around the world and seen for ourselves that people are sinners. Of course, we can do that but the sinners always turn out to be other people. Rather, it is because of what happened on Calvary all those years ago that we can, and must, acknowledge that in the presence of God we have no standing except as forgiven sinners. I think that it is utterly essential to state that first, otherwise all other attempts to talk about sin puts us in the position of being judges of others.

The most systematic account of the matter is the long section in St Paul's letter to the Romans (Chapters 1–7). It is after that wonderful sentence which begins, 'I am not ashamed of the gospel, because it is the power of God for the salvation of everyone who believes' (Romans 1:16) that Paul invites his readers to take a look at the world. No doubt with their full agreement, he paints a picture of that pagan world where all around there was depravity, licentiousness, fighting, quarrelling, warring factions and endemic corruption.

No doubt there would be many, especially among his Jewish readers, who would wholeheartedly agree. But he later turns upon his Jewish readers and declares in words to this effect: 'You who judge others, what about you?' (Romans 2:1). And relentlessly he convicts them of the same types of sin and finally sums up that whole section, beginning with the first part of chapter 3, with a series of quotations from the Psalms which ultimately affirm, 'There is no-one righteous, not even one' (Romans 3:10). We all bear the same condemnation.

When he set out to examine what was at the root of that awful situation, he did not, as so many pagan thinkers did, identify the essence of sin in such things as sexual immorality, sensuality, pride or dissenting factions. No, all of the things he describes are the fruit of a root that is fundamentally unbelief. We have become corrupt because collectively we turned our backs on the Creator and failed to trust him, instead putting our trust in things that were made. And that is a faithful rendering of the story as we have it in Genesis 3.

The essence of the story of the Fall, as it is told in that chapter, is that God called upon his created family of Adam and Eve to live simply in love and obedience and to trust him to do what was good for them. When he forbade them the fruit of that tree, the knowledge of good and evil, the essence of the temptation to which they fell was contained in the words, '…you will be like God, knowing good and evil' (Genesis 3:5). In other words, do not just take it on trust but find out for yourself and make sure that you yourself know what is right or wrong. Do not take it on trust from anybody else.

That, says our Bible, is the root from which all the terrible harvest of sin ultimately comes. It is the breaking of the relationship of love, obedience and trust for which we were created, and the attempt to be our own masters and judges and to have a righteousness of our own. This is why Paul identifies the heart of the gospel as being the gift of a righteousness from God – a righteousness that is not my possession, but God's gift. That is the heart of what Paul has to say about the root, the origin, of human sin and this explains what he would later say about the righteousness of God.

Then in Romans 5–6 Paul goes on to speak about our solidarity in sin. As in Adam all died, so in Christ shall all be made alive. In Adam we all sin. That statement, of our solidarity in sin, has been grievously misunderstood. This is partly because of some words of St Augustine. There are two points to notice here. First of all, in that crucial verse which says that death passed from Adam to all people, in that all sinned (Romans 5:12), the Greek words for 'in that' can, and have been, easily misunderstood or misprinted as 'in whom' – as though the sin of Adam automatically made us all guilty, which is a meaningless concept.

The true text, and all later theologians agree on this, means that it is *because, in that* we have all sinned that we are in solidarity with Adam. Secondly, Augustine disastrously connected this with Psalm 51:5 (KJV): 'and in sin did my mother conceive me'. When read in the context of the psalm this is simply a vivid way of saying, 'I am a sinner from the very beginning.' It does not mean that sin is transmitted through the act of sexual intercourse, but Augustine came close to saying something like it. And this is another misunderstanding that has distorted Western thinking on the doctrine of original sin.

What St Paul was saying – and what we surely have to recognise as truth – is that apart from conscious, individual sins resulting from our deliberate choice, we are all together, as human beings, involved in a sinful network of relationships in which we become victims of sin from the very beginning. This doctrine of original sin is something many people find abhorrent and distasteful and regard as a form of treason or breach of faith against humanity.

But any parent coping with a small child having tantrums because he or she cannot get what they want understands very well what is meant by original sin! We are all together in this network of sinful relationships which existed before we were born, and into which we are born. We are incorporated within it in the way we are brought up. We are all in this together. It is the human condition.

What is the answer to this? The answer is a righteousness from God by faith, as expressed in that fundamental verse (Romans 5:17). To put it another way, it is the gift of a relationship. It is not the gift, as it were, of a new being to ourselves as individuals. It is the gift of a new relationship to replace the one that we have broken. And here, I think, it is so tremendously important to repeat again that all our thinking has been very much shaped by the Greek conception of substance. This is the idea that behind everything that we know, or think we know, there is a kind of underlying substance which is the thing itself, and that everything, including all people and human nature, is to be understood in terms of that which is its essential substance.

But the truth, as it is in the Bible, is otherwise. The truth to be found within the Bible is that what we are constituted by are relationships. We are human beings by virtue of the fact that we are related, that we are children of God. We are all the brothers and sisters, the parents and children, of one another. Human nature does not exist except in a pattern of relationships. These relationships are intrinsic to humankind.

To make clear what I mean, consider this illustration from physics. We all know that for centuries scientists and thinkers had sought to identify the atom as the essential unit of matter, beyond which it was not possible to go. The atom was the ultimate substance underlying all matter. We now know that the atom is not just the smallest particle of a chemical element but part of a network of dynamic relationships between particles which are not themselves matter, but electrical charges. So even matter itself ultimately consists of a pattern of intricate relationships. At the other end of the cosmic scale when we use the word 'God' we are not, properly speaking, referring to some kind of divine substance. We are instead more truthfully and accurately referring to a pattern of relationships between Father, Son and Holy Spirit in complete and absolute love and communion. This is the proper designation of the word 'God'.

From this point of view we can see that the Fall is essentially the attempt by human beings, whose only reality lies in their relationship of dependence upon God, to establish a reality for themselves. This, so to speak, enables them to stand on their own feet in relation to God and to make up their own minds on good and evil and not simply exist in a relationship of love and obedience to the Creator.

That is why the answer to the appalling fact of sin is precisely the establishment of a new relationship: a righteousness from God by faith. This does not involve a righteousness which is mine so that I can say I am a righteous person, but is of a different kind of righteousness. It is a righteousness that comprises the fact that God has accepted us in Jesus Christ and that in faith we believe and accept. It is that relationship between holy God and sinful us which constitutes the only righteousness that there can ever be.

How has this been brought about? First of all we need to look at the Old Testament background to the story told in the Gospels. The Old Testament is full of terrible accounts of the wickedness of human beings, from the first family where one brother murders the other to all those evil acts that finally caused God to try to wipe out the whole world in a flood, preserving only a righteous remnant. Again he destroyed the Tower of Babel when the human family attempted to establish its own authority with a tower that reached up to heaven.

In a sense the whole theme of the Old Testament can be described as God's response – the 'passion of God'. It is the passion of a holy God over his sinful family. It begins with that terrible cry in the Garden of Eden on that first evening when God called out for Adam, 'Where are you?' (Genesis 3:9). It is the agonised cry of a parent whose child has gone astray and is lost.

Throughout the Old Testament there is this passion of God calling upon a family to leave its home, to leave the things that are seen and relied upon and to learn to live a new life simply by faith. That family had been safeguarded and rescued out of slavery in Egypt and brought into a good and pleasant land, but that family defiled this land with their sin and rebelled time and again against their loving Creator. God, in his agony, sometimes threatened them with dreadful punishments, sometimes putting his family under terrible disciplines and then again repenting and wooing its members like a lover pursuing his bride. This is seen in that marvellous passage in Hosea: 'How can I give you up, Ephraim ... all my compassion is aroused' (Hosea 11:8).

Then you have those marvellous passages in the latter part of Isaiah, the so-called 'servant songs', which picture the servant of the Lord – which should have been Israel if it had been true to its calling – as bearing all the sin of the world in that servant's own heart. Finally, we come to our Lord himself in whom all these prophecies signalling the passion of God are made flesh and blood in the life of this human being, Jesus Christ. We see him calling Israel to fulfil the purpose for which it was called – to be God's servant people for all the nations. When that calling was denied, Jesus went alone to his cross to bear in his own body and soul the passion of God for this sinful world.

So the one who is Lord of all was humiliated, cursed, cast out and executed as a criminal and blasphemer. And in his agony and desolation he cried out, 'My God, my God, why have you forsaken me' (Matthew 27:46). Entering right into the God-forsaken state of this sinful family of God, descending into the very depths so that nothing of God's creation might be left unredeemed, God raised him from the dead to a new life and exalted him to heaven as Lord. He sent forth the Holy Spirit on the day of Pentecost to fill the church with the knowledge that this crucified man, rejected by the world, was the mighty God and the Lord of all. And so the church sets forth on its mission to proclaim the mystery of salvation.

What I am trying to explain is that what happened is a fact. God's victory is to be considered an actuality before we begin to advance our theories on how to explain it. It is a fact of history that these things occurred. In the outpouring of the Holy Spirit after the ascension of Jesus, the church was given the assurance and authority to preach to the world that the power of sin had been broken. The righteousness of God had been given to us so that we, the unholy, might live in the love and fellowship of the holy God.

I am absolutely sure that when we speak of the atonement wrought in Jesus Christ we are talking of things that go beyond human language, because language is simply not up to the job of explaining or articulating something which is ultimately the contradiction of all reason, and that is the concept of sin. If we could, as it were, incorporate sin into a coherent rational structure of thought, it would no longer be sin. We are dealing with an 'ultimate', a 'surd', something which simply cannot be apprehended by linguistic or even mathematical structures and fitted into any rational scheme. All our attempts to comprehend what was done through the atonement, in terms of fully thought out conceptual patterns, must therefore fall short of the truth. These attempts, however, can point us towards the truth.

One of the great metaphors of reconciliation used in the Scriptures is the notion of ransom which often depicts the redeeming of a slave from his or her master through the generosity of another. It is an image used by our Lord himself. This metaphor was charged with enormous emotional weight in a society where slavery was so common. But if you try to push this metaphor to its logical conclusion, the question arises, 'To whom was the ransom paid?' Some early theologians suggested it was paid to God while others insisted it went to the devil. But neither can be accepted because to argue that it was a ransom paid to God implies that God had to be placated in order to forgive us. And that would assume that there was antagonism between the Son and the Father, which is wholly contrary to the Christian faith. To argue that it was paid to the devil overstates Satan's authority.

Another metaphor is that of substitution – of another who has died in our place. This again embraces a deep and intrinsic element of truth. And yet it cannot finally explain what happened. It is so clear in the teachings of our Lord himself that while he goes before us, and it is he alone who can meet the ultimate enemy in that final battle, we are not excused from that encounter. It is precisely the opposite – that we may be enabled to follow him, to take up the cross and go the way that he has gone.

There is next the metaphor of sacrifice. This is fully developed in the letter to the Hebrews which so clearly fulfils the Old Testament regulations with regard to sacrifice. We see Jesus as the ultimate sacrifice to the Father. But, once again, we must be careful not to understand or express this as if antagonism existed between the Son and the Father, as though the Father needed to be placated.

It is one of the significant little features of the Old Testament use of the word 'expiation' or 'atonement' that the Hebrew verb, constantly used in relation to God, is never used in the form which puts God as the object. It is used, for example, where Jacob wanted to placate Esau, who was on his way to meet him with an armed band, and Jacob sent a collection of gifts ahead of him. There the word was used as he tried to placate his brother, but it was never used with God as its object. We find that it is always used in a subtle, indirect form – that God has provided a sacrifice, to make atonement concerning sin – so that there is no question of the Son, as it were, placating the Father. On the contrary, the atoning work of Christ is also the work of the Father.

Although we can never fully explain the atonement by using human language, all these different metaphors nevertheless help us get a little closer to the centre of this mystery. I have often said that one of the most helpful of them, is the one concerning the Old Testament Hebrew word for the 'mercy seat', the place where the sinner could be received by the holy God. This is translated in Romans 3 as the 'place of propitiation'. Surely here we come near to the heart of what was done there. It has created a place where we who are sinners, and we are still sinners, can nevertheless be in fellowship with God who is holy, because in this act the Son of God, in loving obedience to the Father, has taken his place right where we are in our lost state. He has therefore made possible a *koinonia*, a communion, in the Holy Spirit, in which we share the very life of God himself, sinners though we are.

This word *koinonia* which we translate as 'fellowship', the fellowship of the Holy Spirit, is actually a word which means common sharing in a property. If I and three brothers jointly own a field it would be said that we had *koinonia* in that field. When we refer to the fellowship of the Holy Spirit we are speaking of a shared participation in the actual life of God the Holy Spirit. That place, of course, is the church. This is where we gather in the name of Jesus. We hear his words, and in the sacrament which he has ordained, we partake of his dying and his victorious resurrection and triumph over death. This is the place where we know and experience justification and sanctification.

Justification is being recognised by God. This is not because we are in ourselves just, or righteous, but because in this act in Jesus Christ he has accepted us as just, as righteous. It is a righteousness which is on the one hand the sheer gift of God and on the other hand is accepted in faith. It is never our possession, but something received moment by moment, by faith in what God has done for us in Jesus Christ.

It is also the place of sanctification. Again, this does not mean that sanctification is a process by which we gradually become holy in ourselves, as though we could obtain a holiness which was not simply God's gift, but was our personal characteristic. That would be a contradiction at the very heart of the gospel. It is interesting to note that when Paul puts the words for justification and sanctification together it is sanctification which comes first: 'You were washed, you were sanctified, you were justified ... ' (1 Corinthians 6:11). Both the words sanctification and justification refer to a relationship with God, not to something that we possess within ourselves. The holiness which is the proper mark of a disciple of Jesus is not, and can never be, something that we possess in that way. So we can never assert that perfect holiness, something which was so central to John Wesley's preaching in the eighteenth century is, so to speak, a designation, a kind of personal possession. That perfect holiness is simply the relationship of faithful dependence upon the sanctifying grace of God.

It seems to me that this all adds up to a most joyful way of preaching the doctrine of original sin. G. K. Chesterton, that quick witted and provocative English critic, novelist and poet, talked about 'the good news of original sin'. What did he mean by that? Let me put it in a rather jocular way. If the whole lot of us are nothing more than a bunch of escaped convicts, which by analogy is what we are, then there is room for an enormous amount of joy, of celebration of being alive and of much merriment in the life of the church. We do not have to go around pretending to be righteous. We have no place at all except as forgiven sinners who have been embraced, accepted and loved by the holy God. And as the Psalms so often remind us, this is something which can only lead us onwards to singing and dancing.

We are delivered from the unbearable burden of trying to be ourselves, wrapped up in our own righteousness. We have one thing and one thing only to do, to believe and to give our lives in a moment by moment offering of thanks to the one who loves us and who laid down his life for us. And that is what the Christian life is. Yes, it's good news!

8 THE CHURCH: ONE, HOLY, APOSTOLIC

In the previous chapter I referred to one of the ways in which St Paul spoke about what was done on the cross when he used the Greek word which translates the Old Testament Hebrew word for the 'mercy seat'. In the New Testament the word is translated as 'propitiation'. One of the most helpful ways to comprehend what Christ did for us on the cross lies in the knowledge and understanding that he has created a place where sinful men and women, despite their sins, may be accepted by God and enabled to live and rejoice in his presence. It is, if you like, the continuation of the ministry of Jesus who received sinners and ate and drank with them. The church is the place where this still happens.

The church is obviously an integral part of the gospel. Nobody becomes a Christian by first of all studying the doctrines of atonement and justification by faith, and so forth, and then at the end of the 'course' looking around for some place to make contact. On the contrary, we become Christians because in one way or another the work of the Holy Spirit has drawn us into some kind of existing Christian fellowship. The church precedes our faith, and as always, the gospel is not a set of disembodied ideas or a set of words. It is always a concrete reality in history: a reality which we call the church.

The New Testament word for the church is the Greek word *ekklesia*, which also means 'assembly', and from which words such as ecclesiastical and so forth are derived. And it is worth looking at the background of that word. The Bible of the early church was the Greek of what we call the Old Testament. In it they would have read of the congregation, the whole assembly, of the people of Israel. These Old Testament meanings were rendered in the Greek by two words – *synagogos* and *ekklesia*. They might have taken either *synagogos* or *ekklesia* because they understood themselves to be the congregation which had its origin in God's calling of Abraham. They did not see themselves as a new society. They were the congregation of the people of Israel which was enlarged to include the Gentiles, as God had promised to both the patriarchs and prophets.

They could, as I have said, chosen either of those two words. There is one place in the New Testament where the word synagogue, *synagogos*, is used, but otherwise they always used the other word *ekklesia*, which the Greek Old Testament uses. And perhaps there were two reasons for that. One might be that the word synagogue was already used by the Jews for their congregations. The other was that the word *ekklesia* was a secular word which described the assembly of all the people.

In the Greek city states the affairs of the city were settled in the assembly, as we see in the latter chapters of Acts, and that assembly was called the *ekklesia*, the calling out of the people. That is its literal meaning. In Acts the assembly was called by what we would now refer to as the town clerk and all the citizens were expected to attend. But this is the assembly called, not by the town clerk, but by God. And so the church is constantly referred to in the Greek as *ekklesia tou Theou*, the assembly of God, the assembly which God called. That was the phrase the first Christians used to describe their togetherness as the continuation of the congregation of the people of Israel.

This explains an important little point in the New Testament – that the same name is used both for an individual local church and for the church as a whole. We ourselves tend to use two words. We use the term 'congregation' when we speak of a local gathering and we are inclined to use the word 'church' for the universal body. But the early church had no such distinction. You will notice this in the Acts and in Paul's letters. He speaks of the churches of Asia, or the church of Asia. It is not that the individual churches are branches of the church. The church is that act of God gathering his people in each place, and in all places. So it is necessary to have this dynamic picture, which is the real inner meaning of this biblical language.

Everywhere God is gathering his people through Jesus Christ into this place of atonement where it is possible for sinful men and women to have fellowship with God. But that action is happening both locally and universally. And that is also why the church is never designated by any other adjectives except the name of the place and the name of the one who calls it.

It is the assembly of God in Corinth, the assembly of God in Ephesus, the congregation of God in Colossae. That is how the church is defined. It is defined by the one who calls it and by where this calling takes place.

When it was proposed to call the church by any name other than the name of God and the name of the place – as, for example, in Corinth (1 Corinthians 3), where people said we are of Peter's party, of Apollos' or Paul's party – Paul was scandalised. He effectively said, 'You are carnal. You have dismembered the body of Christ.' Paul was affronted by the thought that anyone should attach any name except that of Christ and the place.

So the church in each place is the catholic church, the universal church, and not a branch. It is the catholic church because God is here calling it. And where God is, you cannot say that it is a branch of a church; it is *the* church. This means that by its very nature, the church is one. There is one God and one Lord Jesus Christ, and there is one place of atonement, not many, and therefore the church is one. But here, of course, we come to the sad story of disunity. We know that the church throughout its history has become divided.

It is worthwhile running over the main divisions. The first great partition happened in the fourth and fifth centuries when the churches outside the Roman Empire, which could not take part in the theological discussions that defined the nature of Christ, became separated. I am thinking, for example, of the Armenians, Assyrians, Syrians, Copts and Ethiopians, many of whom would probably never have become separated but for that tremendous political divide.

You can well understand that when the Roman and Persian empires were either at war or in a state of political hostility, Christians in Persia, Armenia or India might well have been suspected of being stooges of the ruling empire. If you lived in the Roman empire these people were regarded as foreigners. So although there were doctrinal differences, this was principally a politically motivated division, which has left us with what we call the 'lesser eastern churches'.

The second great division came in the eleventh century with the mutual excommunications of Byzantium and Rome. The two halves of the Empire had been drifting apart for a long time, but it is important to remember that from the point of view of the eastern churches the Roman Catholic Church was, for two reasons, a schismatic body.

First the Roman church made an addition to the Nicene creed without consulting the whole body of the church. They added the so-called 'Filioque clause': the words, 'and from the Son'. This related to whether the Holy Spirit proceeds from the Father (which both churches agreed upon) *as well as* the Son. This still remains a deeply resented schismatic act in the minds of eastern Christians. The second reason was the action of Pope Leo III in crowning Charlemagne in St Peter's Church on Christmas Day in AD 800 as emperor when there was already an emperor on the throne in Constantinople. These two theological and political acts were seen as schismatic. To this day in the Eastern part of Christendom – in the Russian, Greek, Serbian and other major orthodox churches – there remains a deep sense of resentment against the Church of Rome. In some ways this division goes much deeper than that within the Western church – between the Roman Catholics and the churches of the Reformation.

In the sixteenth century the third division occurred, with which we are all so familiar: the Reformation which separated Northern and Southern Europe from each other. And then in the nineteenth century, especially in the United States, the idea of a denomination developed, as though Christians could quite contentedly live in separate bodies, regarding themselves all as different branches of the same church. That was the fourth major point of schism to further divide the church.

How are we to understand the issues that divided the church? I suppose it is helpful to draw attention to three great emphases that are not mutually contradictory – which are all properly part of the reality of the church – but have become separated and put against one another. I am speaking of what one might roughly call the Catholic, the Protestant and the Pentecostal emphases.

Look first at the Catholic emphasis. Jesus said to his disciples, 'You did not choose me, but I chose you ...' (John 15:16). The church is not a body of people who have decided that they are going to follow Jesus. The church is that body created by Jesus. He called them apostles, consecrating them and sending them out into the world to make disciples of all nations. It was a specific and particular body historically created, formed and sent forth by Jesus Christ. He gave them the sacraments of baptism and the Lord's Supper, and they went out and preached. Subsequently they appointed their successors from those among the believers they found to be fit for that office.

The emphasis here is that the church exists not as a body which we have created or constituted. It is there as the body which Jesus Christ himself sent into the world. But some people set themselves up and say, 'We will have our own leadership. We have consecrated our own bishops and we will do our own thing.' Is that the church? Surely the church is something that is given, with its objective reality, which we must clearly embrace if we are to find salvation. That is the Catholic emphasis.

One of the most vivid expressions of this emphasis is to be found in the autobiography of John Henry Newman, the great Anglican leader, who in 1845 became a Roman Catholic and led many others to follow him. If you read the autobiography of this writer, poet and historian you will see that this man was passionately concerned with the overriding question: 'Which is the true church?' He reasoned that if one was not part of the true church then one was not saved. As a result of his agonised and reasoned arguments he concluded that the Roman Catholic Church was the true church and that all the others, however excellent, were not the authentic church. So the church is defined, at least in part, by its valid historical succession. It can show that it is the same body which Jesus sent out into the world, not something that has been shaped by any kind of innovation.

Against this you have the tremendous issues that arose so strongly at the time of the Reformation: that the church may well have a valid apostolic succession, but it could lose its way. Its bishops may have been consecrated by bishops who in turn were consecrated by bishops, and so on, until you reach those who were consecrated by the original apostles, and yet it still might fall into error and sin. Episcopal consecration could not guarantee the reality of the church. In the robust language that people used at the time of the Reformation, the Scots reformer John Knox (1505–72) declared, 'Lineal descent is no mark by which the true church may be distinguished from the kirk malignant, that horrible harlot!' Well, theological discussions were conducted in a lively manner in those days, but that was the essential emphasis.

The point the Reformers made was that the church was something created by the action of the living Christ. Its existence did not simply depend upon historic succession but was created by the living power of the gospel, mediated through the word and the sacraments of the gospel. This dynamic conception of the church had enormous power. It brought about a tremendous renewal, but also, of course, a tremendous division in the life of the church. The danger is that it seems to neglect that which the Catholic emphasis affirms. It is in danger of making the church something which, as it were, happens moment by moment, or fails to happen, but not something which is a given historical reality continuing through history.

Next there is what I call the Pentecostal emphasis. You may have correct apostolic succession and correct doctrine as well as properly administered sacraments, and yet the living power of the Spirit may be absent. Are you then the true church? There is a grim little story in the Acts of a man who was claiming to cast out evil spirits in the name of Jesus and Paul, and several demoniacs attacked him, exclaiming, 'Jesus I know and I know about Paul, but who are you?' (Acts 19:15). Do you have the authentic presence of the living Spirit or not?

Each of those three emphases is valid. They have their authentication in the gospel. Yet each, taken alone, can lead to a vital loss of substance. The Catholic emphasis, by itself, can produce something which has no life in it, which is formal and dead. The Protestant emphasis can produce something very lively but which has no sense of unity. It can break apart, especially when the whole thing depends upon correct doctrine. The history of the Protestant church is one of continual division over the detail of doctrine so that the unity of the church disappears from view.

In the Pentecostal tradition the danger is that one emphasises experience, individual personal experience, without paying sufficient attention to these questions: 'What is it we are experiencing? What is the reality with which we are dealing?' In our kind of society, especially with its tendency to subjectivism and relativism, there is a real danger that this emphasis, taken by itself, can lead to the church dissolving into 'what I feel'.

With great respect to our good friends in the Methodist church I think one has to recognise that this dissolving has sometimes happened. John Wesley's great revival saw a tremendous outpouring of the power of the Spirit, manifested in the transformation of lives and in the manifold gifts of the Spirit. But Christianity has often dissolved into something defined as 'what I feel good about' – merely a kind of personal subjective experience. This is because at times insufficient attention has been given both to doctrine – to what we believe, the truth to which we have committed ourselves – and to the given continuity and reality of the universal church. These three elements, integral to the fullness of the gospel, can nevertheless lead us to division and mutual suspicion when they are separated. The result is that we profoundly suspect one another of not being true to the reality of the church.

How can we overcome these divisions? We cannot escape the force of the words our Lord used on the night of his passion, '…that all of them may be one, Father, just as you are in me and I am in you. May they also be in us so that the world may believe…' (John 17:21). We cannot deny that it is the intention of our Lord that the church should be in such ways a visible unity, that the world may recognise that this is the place of atonement where sin is forgiven and where we can be reconciled to one another. This is the place of which Jesus spoke: 'I, when I am lifted up from the earth, will draw all people to myself' (John 12:32). We cannot escape the vital importance of unity, no matter how much we may be disappointed in the face of difficulty.

But let us not forget that we are now living in the first age of Christian reunion. The entire history of the church over the past centuries has been one long story of continual division. We are the privileged ones who live in an age where for the first time people are beginning to come together, though perhaps slowly and hesitantly, and to recognise one another in Christ despite our many differences.

How does God enable us to restore the unity of the church? The problem is that each of us is bound to confess that a church to which he or she belongs is the church of God. This is because that specific church was the one that drew that particular person to Christ. I cannot deny that. And the temptation for us is that we look at one another and perhaps say, 'In this respect you lack something. You lack one of the essential marks of the church.' It might be in regard to doctrine or apostolic succession or in relation to the place of the Spirit in the life of one's church, but we tend to say to each other, 'If you can correct yourself at this point, then we can unite.'

But there is an important difference between asserting that something is a proper mark of the church and maintaining that something is essential to the church. Something can be a proper mark of the church – and these three things I have mentioned are proper marks of the church, they properly belong to the nature of the church – but if you say they are essential, then you are suggesting that without them there is no church. And none of us has been willing to draw the logical conclusion of that.

From the Roman Catholic point of view, in the report of the Anglican Roman Catholic International Commission it is said, for example, that recognition of the Papacy or recognition of a certain doctrine of the Eucharist is 'essential' as a pre-requisite of union. You are really saying that without these there is no church. 'Essential' means exactly that, fundamental or absolutely necessary. The logic of this kind of thinking would be to conclude that those churches which lack these things ought to have disappeared – as a branch cut from the vine perishes – and if a church lacks something essential to its life then it ought not to exist. And all our excommunications of one another, such as the excommunications exchanged between the patriarch of Constantinople and the Pope of Rome in 1054, if God had 'validated' them, would have meant that these churches would have disappeared and thus no longer existed as part of the church. But they have not disappeared.

Surely we must accept the fact that the church exists only by the mercy of God, only by his grace to sinners and not by its fulfilment of any of the conditions for the fullness of the church. It is, as I have suggested, the basic picture of the place of atonement: where God receives sinners into his fellowship. Does that not mean, therefore, that the way for us to restore the unity of the church is that we accept one another as God seems to have accepted us? Let us accordingly accept one another as we are, acknowledging the many ways in which we fall short of God's purpose for the church and then, having accepted one another as we are, seek to correct, reform and build up one another in the faith.

There is a kind of relaxed and tolerant easy-going way, which

I fear is becoming all too popular, which finds expression when we simply say, 'Yes, let us all accept one another, because God has accepted us.' And we leave it at that. It is the equivalent of our saying, 'Shall we go on sinning, so that grace may increase?' (Romans 6:1). If God has given grace to churches which are sinful, which lack something that belongs properly to the church, let us just carry on and God will continue to give us his grace. This notion is unthinkable: 'Shall we continue in sin, that grace may abound?' St Paul's reply is vehement, 'God forbid' (v.2). It is unthinkable. The mercy of God towards churches which lack that which belongs properly to the church, should not lead us to contentment. Rather it should lead us to repentance and to a willingness not merely to accept one another, but to correct one another. We should therefore hold one another up to the reality of the gospel itself so that God may make of us what he intends us to be.

Looking at the present situation, some general points can be made about the church in Europe. If we look at the church in parts of the world such as Africa, Asia and the Pacific Islands where it continues to grow rapidly, the situation is different. But in considering the situation in Europe I think we have to agree that the Roman Catholic Church, with a kind of stubborn intransigence, is still a tremendous power but is nevertheless facing severe internal contradictions and crises.

I think undoubtedly the mainline Protestant churches in Europe are in decline and that the main growing parts of the church in Europe are the evangelical and charismatic bodies, both within the churches and in the various 'parachurch' organisations, fellowships and associations, which are springing up so luxuriantly around us.

At this point it is important to say one word about the importance of the Catholic tradition. When I was a student it was the Anglo-Catholic wing of the Church of England which was strong and vigorous, producing the best scholars, many of the best priests and generally setting the pace. Evangelicals were a relatively small and rather frightened minority. The position today is almost exactly the opposite.

The evangelical wing of the church is strong, growing and confident, and the Catholic wing of the church, especially following the crisis over the admission of women to the priesthood, is on the defensive. And I think that exactly at this point, we recognise the importance of the Catholic tradition, the objective reality of the church and its sacraments as something which is given, and not just a matter of my personal experience.

I have often been a bit turned off when some of my friends have spoken of a Eucharistic service as if the important thing about it was whether or not it had personal meaning, as though essentially it was a kind of subjective experience. If you compare that with what St Paul says in 1 Corinthians about participation in the Eucharist, where he says that if you take part in it without discerning the body, it is not merely that nothing happens, it is that you are under judgment. Whatever happens when you take part in the Eucharist it is not that nothing happens; something happens! (1 Corinthians 11:27–29)

Either you are built up in your life in Christ, or you are judged, but an objective reality exists there. I think it is important that we recover our sense of this in the face of the subjectivism and relativism of so much of our culture. I say this because currently it is the evangelical and charismatic parts of the church which are, thank God, so strong and confident and bearing so much fruit.

I think we are all uncertain about how to proceed in the matter of Christian unity. This is because the movements towards organic unity, so promising around fifty years ago, seem in large measure to have petered out. We have to discover new ways and means to express our unity across the board, from the Roman Catholic and Orthodox churches, to the evangelical and charismatic churches where so much of the main growth is now going on. Perhaps at first these new ways can be very informal. But undoubtedly we are faced with one of the greatest challenges of the present time.

The real issue that divides Christians in the United Kingdom today is not between Catholics and evangelicals or Protestants and charismatics, but the difference between those who believe that there is a gospel and those who have ceased to believe that. On the one hand there are those who believe unequivocally in a God-given reality: 'For God so loved the world, that he gave his one and only Son' (John 3:16), and that here is the place of atonement. I think that Catholics, evangelicals and charismatics have that in common. On the other hand, there are sadly a great many Christians in the United Kingdom who have lost the sense of there being a real God, and have allowed their faith to dissolve away into opinions and subjective experiences, with no real gospel.

Let me finish with five affirmations that sum up what I want to say. The first is the one with which I began: the historic reality of the Christian church. It is important to stress this point because when you listen to the radio, watch television or read the newspapers, you soon realise the church is often regarded as a fairly marginal phenomenon interested only in gaining popularity. The inevitable, and almost only, question the media asks is whether or not certain activities are going to make churches more popular. It is as though they are looked upon as a passing phenomenon and if they are not popular enough they will disappear. How absurd, especially when you remember that the church has outlived mighty empires, infamous totalitarian structures and great philosophical systems. Within twenty years the things that today seem to occupy the whole horizon of public thinking will become half-remembered phantoms, mere ephemera, of a past age. But the church will still be there.

The church is historic reality, beginning with God's call to Abraham and continuing through the ministry of prophets and apostles right down the ages until now. And whether or not the church is popular, big or small, is relatively unimportant. The fact of this great rock, this anvil upon which so many hammers have been worn out, this given reality, needs to be at the centre of our thinking as Christians.

Secondly, the church is a body of sinful men and women. It is a body of sinners whom God calls saints. St Paul usually starts his letters by saying something like this: 'Paul, called to be an apostle to the church in Corinth, called to be saints.' The Greek actually says, 'Called apostle, called saints.' It is not in the Greek, 'Called to *be* saints' it is 'called saints' – *kletos apostolos, kletois hagiois*. In other words, God calls them saints.

They may not look like it but God calls them saints and it is what God calls them that matters. They are sinners! Yes we are! But God calls us saints because God has made us his own – that is the whole meaning of atonement. Of course, the church is always going to be a bunch of sinners. It has never been anything else. And it is very easy to become completely pessimistic about the church. We have to be realistic and not pretend that the church is anything other than it is. But we also have to be faithful, knowing that it is what God says that goes. If God has called us saints, made us his own, given us his gift of atonement in Jesus Christ, then that defines who and what we are.

Above all, let us not escape with this idea of an invisible church. The invisible church is an attractive idea because the visible church is the people God has chosen, and as we know, he has chosen some pretty funny characters. The invisible church has the great advantage that 'I' choose who belongs to it. It is the church of the people that I think are the real Christians and that, of course, is very comforting, but that is not the church. The church is that body of sinners, whom God has called and chosen to be saints, to belong to him.

Thirdly, the church is defined by its centre, not by its boundaries. When you begin to define the church by its boundaries, you get into all kinds of legalistic difficulties: 'Was that person baptised? Was the one who baptised that person ordained by a bishop? Was that bishop consecrated in the apostolic succession? Was the right statement of faith signed? Did the person concerned have the right kind of spiritual experience?' These are all relevant questions but the ultimate questions are: 'Is he or she absolutely committed to Christ? Is Christ absolutely fundamental for him or her?' By that I mean Christ as he is known to us in the Scriptures, not a Christ that we imagine.

I am afraid there are many people who talk about Christ, but not about the Christ we meet in the Gospels. They talk of an ideal figure they have manufactured for themselves. I am talking about the Christ who is known to us in the Gospels. We know what he said and did and we know what he calls us to do.

Essentially I believe the church is constituted by its relationship to Jesus Christ. If a person tells me that for him or her, Jesus is final and decisive, then I must regard that person as a brother or sister in Christ. From that point, I can begin to ask, 'Then how do you reconcile what you do with Jesus? How can you reconcile what you say with Jesus?' There is a basis on which we can correct one another and build one another up, but it is the centre that defines the whole thing.

The fourth point is that the church is a sign and an instrument – a foretaste of the kingdom of God. The church is not itself the kingdom of God, nor is the kingdom something completely separate from the church. When we separate the kingdom of God from the church, then the church becomes some kind of ideology, a sort of programme or a social or political utopia. The church is both the sign and the instrument, and therefore the foretaste. It is a sign, and a sign always points away from itself. If you are in Manchester you will not see a sign pointing to Manchester. It is when you are elsewhere that you have a sign. So the church is a sign in that it points to something which is not itself but is a foretaste of the reality of God's reign. It is a guiding light or it may be an instrument in the hands of God for doing his will in the world, an instrument of the kingdom. It is both of those because it is a foretaste. The church is that fellowship within which we enjoy a foretaste of the freedom, the joy, the holiness of God's kingdom. And because it is a taste or experience of something to be enjoyed in advance, it can be looked upon as both a sign and an instrument.

My fifth and final point is that the church – and this is the proper sense of the invisible church – is in communion with the saints who have gone before. This is an element that we are in danger of losing in the reformed Protestant churches. We must not lose this most precious thing, that the churches remain in communion with those who have gone before us on the way of faith, who wait with us for the final victory of Christ, for the resurrection of the body and the coming of the new heavens and new earth.

It ought to be a living part of our life in Christ, that we share in the communion of the saints, in the fellowship of those who have gone before us and who inspire us as they, and we, look to Jesus and to his final victory, of which we have the foretaste, right now, in the gift of the Holy Spirit.

9 THE LAST THINGS: THE KINGDOM OF GOD

The Bible is a story. It is the story of all things, from the beginning to the end. It is a faithful account of the Creation, the making of all things. It is also a narrative of the Fall, which alienated our world from its Creator. It is a recital of God's redeeming work and of that consummation he has promised.

We are now approaching a discussion of the 'last things' – death, resurrection, immortality, the end of the world and final judgment – what is technically called 'eschatology'. This term is derived from the Greek word *eschatos* which means the end. Theologians love to throw around words like eschatology, perhaps to remind us of their scholarship and erudition. So just in case you might want to sound a little more learned in your next conversation, I offer this one quite freely – for what it's worth!

There is nothing more significant and decisive for moulding and defining our way of understanding than the story that we tell of ourselves. It is pivotal. Europe has been defined and characterised by its own story which has made it distinct from Asia. But, of course, the account that Europeans have given of themselves over these past two hundred years has not been the story of the Bible, but rather of what we have chosen to call 'progress'. This doctrine of 'progress', which has its origins in the eighteenth century, has shaped our thinking from the middle of the eighteen century until the First World War. To a large extent, we are still immersed in it. We find it difficult to view this cult of progress with detachment and often fail to shake our minds out of it and to recognise that it is a very recent story. It is a story culturally unknown in many parts of the world, and it is certainly not the story the Bible tells.

It is this reverence of 'progress' which causes us to think automatically that the things and events of earlier times are crude, primitive and less developed. We habitually and mechanically believe that the things of the present and future are, and always will be, more refined and better developed. We unconsciously think that everything old fashioned and out of date is by definition inferior. This whole mode of thinking is expressed in words like progress, development, evolution, growth and so forth. We have been conditioned into thinking of our story in those terms, as a continuous upward movement. C. S. Lewis aptly termed this phenomenon 'chronological snobbery' – that anything modern or recent is always better than something ancient.

At the same time, there is another, older story which still persists in the back of our minds. This is about how things were somehow much better in the past. It is a story told especially by old people, but a very familiar story. This is also an ancient story which suggests the idea of a golden age in the past. Human history is felt to be a journey of descent from that golden age to the present.

In society today much depends upon the relative importance between the old and the young. In most traditional societies the old are supposed to be wise and their point of view is respected. But with the rise of the doctrine of progress in the eighteenth century, as a direct result of the Enlightenment and the Age of Reason, a conscious movement arose throughout Europe to take the education of the young out of the hands of parents and churches. A system of government-controlled state education was developed that inculcated into successive generations a different view of the world.

The whole idea that education should be the responsibility of the government is a very recent concept and is one of the implications of that new doctrine of progress.

Behind both these stories there is a still more ancient one, perhaps the most popular, which combines the idea of progress with that of a golden age in the past. And that is to see life and nature as a circle, a continuous and inexorable wheel, where things rise, develop, mature, decay and finally fall. It is, of course, a natural way of understanding ourselves because it is what we always see in the natural world around us. Plants and animals, everything in the natural world, is seen to go through a changing cycle. There is a time for renewal and growth, then of maturity leading to decay. But then another cycle begins, so that we have the feeling that we are moving, but in fact we are going nowhere because ultimately we are part of this great turning wheel of nature.

The most rigorous development of this worldview is found in Indian thought with the fundamental concept of reincarnation. None of the great religious movements – Buddhism, Sikhism, the modern religious movements in India – has questioned the idea of reincarnation. The different schools of thought in Hinduism represent different proposals for escaping from this endless, meaningless cycle of birth and rebirth. Escaping from this appalling and terrible prospect – of ceaseless birth and rebirth, where in each incarnation we are compelled to suffer the consequences of the deeds of our previous life – forms the background of all Indian religion.

One of the extraordinary ironies of today is that significant numbers of people in the Western world are trying to revive belief in the idea of reincarnation. They would thus imprison themselves on that eternal wheel from which Indian religion has spent all its energies in trying to escape. It is one of the stark illustrations of the fact that if the story of the Bible no longer guides and directs us, we shall return inevitably to Asia and become, again, simply the western end of Asia.

But, of course, the story we have told over the past two hundred years, the way of understanding our history as a chronicle of progress and development, has this one fatal flaw: we shall not be around at the end. However much we might think of history in terms of a glorious future for the human race, one thing is quite certain – we shall not be there. This has inevitably resulted in the separation of our vision of the future of society from that of our personal future.

That is the root of the privatisation of religion about which we often complain. If for the sake of argument the real meaning of history were to be realised in the year 20,000, when we shall not be alive, then we have to ask about the goal of personal history, and that then becomes a separate issue. It becomes the idea of a personal survival of death, because one has dropped out of the history of the world. So we have this dividing of these two eschatologies – the public and the private – and there seems to be no way of bringing them together because inevitably one has dropped out of the story of the world before it has been completed.

What is unique about the eschatology of the Bible – the vision of the end which we have in Revelation, the last book of the Bible – is that it draws together and unites the public and private. It is the holy city into which the kings of the earth bring their glory. It is therefore the consummation of the whole history of civilisation, because the literal meaning of the one civilisation is the making of a city. It is all these things, but it is also the consummation of every personal life. It is the place where the tears will be wiped from each and every eye and where we shall be with God and see him face to face.

How is it that the Bible is able to bring together that which we have split asunder in our telling of the story? The answer is that since it was sin and death that created the split, it is sin and death that separates us from the human story before it reaches its end. It is only because the Bible tells the story of how sin and death have been conquered that it can give us an eschatology which includes both the public and private. To put it very crudely and bluntly, we see that the end does not come as the result of a smooth and upward progress, but only after judgment and catastrophe: the fire of judgment that burns everything. In other words, only after the cross comes the resurrection.

Consider the biblical understanding of the end. Take a look at it as a whole. If we examine the Old Testament we know that its great central theme is that the Lord reigns. The Lord who delivered us out of slavery in Egypt is the Lord of heaven and earth and in the end all nations and all peoples will acknowledge him. But overwhelmingly, the Old Testament sees the end as something which is in this world. It is a picture of a renewed world. 'Every valley shall be raised up, every mountain and hill made low' (Isaiah 40:4); 'The wolf will live with the lamb, the leopard will lie down with the goat ... and a little child will lead them' (Isaiah 11:6); 'Everyone will sit under their own vine and under their own fig tree, and no-one will make them afraid' (Micah 4:4). All these pictures in the Old Testament of the promised end are pictures in this world. It is true that there are hints of something beyond death, not strongly developed but nevertheless present.

The events of the Maccabean wars seems to have made the decisive difference. In the struggle to overcome the appalling tyranny of the pagan rule of the Greek emperors, thousands of loyal Jews were slain because they faithfully and courageously refused to break the Sabbath by fighting on that day. It became impossible to believe that all these unfortunate people who perished in faith should be excluded from the consummation for which they had fought and died. It is therefore in this inter-testamental period that the doctrine of the resurrection of the dead came to occupy a key place in Jewish thinking. But as we know from the New Testament, not all Jews accepted this.

The Sadducees declined to accept the doctrine of resurrection because they had made a cosy and comfortable concordat with the ruling power and were prepared to let things go on as they were. The doctrine of resurrection was most decidedly a revolutionary and subversive doctrine because it implied that things, as they stood, were not the last word. We know that on this issue Jesus sided decisively with the Pharisees and against the Sadducees, and taught the resurrection of the body.

At the time of Jesus himself the Holy Land had for centuries past been desecrated by pagan armies, the Temple desecrated, the Law flouted, the rule of God denied and his people subjugated to the humiliation of slavery. It was a time of smouldering fomentation beneath the surface, always leading to the question: 'How long do we have to wait before God intervenes to fulfil his promises?'

We know from the Gospels that Jesus in his own person knew himself to be the presence of the rule and kingdom of God. The central message he brought to the world was that the rule of God was at hand. The hour had come. The crucial moment of judgment and redemption had arrived.

It is clear that to begin with Jesus sought to summon the people of Israel as a whole to recognise the presence of this hour of judgment. They were urged to recognise the signs of the times and to fulfil the vocation for which God had called them: to be the suffering servant who manifested the glory of the kingdom of God. When Israel rejected this call, Jesus in a multitude of parables and teachings, warned that the absolute destruction of Israel was imminent. Here one thinks in particular of the parable of the tenants (Matthew 21:33–46). And with that destruction would come the crisis for the world. It is clear, however, that Jesus knew that in the end it was he himself, and he alone, who could and would fulfil the calling of Israel. That fulfilment would take place as he alone heeded God's call to be his servant, to suffer and to bear the sin of the world. He accordingly began to teach his disciples that he must suffer and die, but would rise again. And as we know, this is what actually happened.

But things did not turn out exactly as devout Jews thought they would. The resurrection of Jesus was not the end of history. The disciples at first thought it ought to be. They asked him, 'Lord, are you at this time going to restore the kingdom to Israel?' (Acts 1:6). They wanted to know if they were to have the kingdom then and there. If not, what was the meaning and point of all these things that had happened?

But Jesus told them they would have to wait. The day of final judgment was in the hands of the Father. But there would be a space, an interval of time between the resurrection of Jesus and the final end. There would be a time for the gospel to be disseminated throughout all nations, a time to repent and prepare for the day of judgment. How long that time would be the Father alone knew.

The disciples were taught to understand that they had been entrusted with the secret of the resurrection, that the death of Jesus was not the defeat of God's kingdom. On the contrary it was the victory. So this delay of the final judgment was to allow time for the gospel to be preached to all nations and to give them time to repent. As to the length of the delay, it was not for them to know. Jesus said, 'No-one knows about that day or hour, not even the angels in heaven, nor the Son, but only the Father' (Matthew 24:36).

What Jesus says of that momentous day is both that it is immediate and yet its timing is uncertain. There are parables and sayings of Jesus which suggest the end is imminent. Others stress the need for patience – there is no certain day.

Time and again, Jesus makes use of the image of the watchman. His job is to stay awake and alert throughout the night, and for hour after hour nothing might happen. But suddenly the decisive moment arrives when the master appears and all have to be ready immediately. So it is this combination of alertness and patience which corresponds to the fact that the final day is immediate, and yet at the same time we do not know when it will be.

Many modern New Testament scholars have looked only at those sayings of Jesus which speak of the immediacy and have then concluded that since two thousand years have passed, Jesus was simply mistaken. But this is the result of reading only half of the evidence. Indeed, it is extraordinary to me that contemporary New Testament scholars talk almost unanimously in this way. This is despite the fact that it is impossible to understand why the early church continued to spread the words and sayings of Jesus when they supposedly already knew or suspected that he was fundamentally mistaken.

What does the gospel teach us of the understanding of the end? I think it is summed up most beautifully in that verse at the beginning of the first letter of Peter: 'Praise be to the God and Father of our Lord Jesus Christ! In his great mercy he has given us new birth into a living hope through the resurrection of Jesus Christ from the dead, and into an inheritance that can never perish, spoil or fade – kept in heaven for you' (1 Peter 1:3–4). Those words are a wonderful summary of what has been accomplished.

There is a sense of hope which is not simply expressed as the desire for something in the future, which may or may not occur, but which we very much want to happen. It is not hope in that weak and vague sense which we so often use, but hope in the sense of absolute confidence: eagerly awaiting something that is assured, even though we do not know the day of its coming. In the words of the letter to the Hebrews, it is a hope that is 'an anchor for the soul' (Hebrews 6:19). It is unshakeable in its solidity. That is what we have been given. The resurrection of Jesus Christ is the pledge that death and sin have been conquered. We know that the end is the victory of God in Jesus Christ.

We must understand the future in a different way. Our contemporary model of understanding the future has been around for the past two centuries or so. It attempts to paint a picture of a solid future, a future of hoped for continuing progress, rather than to suggest that we are peering into an essentially unknown future. But whatever the skills and technological wizardry of our computer-aided forecasters, all that we really know is that we do not know the future. It can always be a total surprise. What we look forward to in the Christian vocabulary is not 'future' but 'advent': that someone is coming to meet us. The horizon of our acting and thinking is thus not some unknown future, some utopia in perhaps the thirtieth or fortieth century. Its perspective is not my own personal survival, but the coming of Jesus. That is what we look forward to, that is the model, that is our horizon.

What do we envisage when we look to the future? What vista of an imagined future lies before us? Without doubt the answer is that momentous image of Jesus coming as the bearer of God's final victory and judgment. This means that our actions are not, so to speak, to be understood as creating or building the kingdom of God, as people used to say a few decades ago. It is not that our actions directly fulfil God's purpose for history as a whole. We know that our actions are ambivalent, confused and contradictory, and that even our good intentions often lead to results quite different from what was intended. No, the meaning of our actions should be understood essentially as 'acted prayers' for the kingdom. We pray, 'Your kingdom come.' But our actions are simply those prayers put into action, and they are offered to God to make of them what he will in his own providential design.

None of the geometrical patterns that I mentioned at the beginning is a satisfactory model. There is the cyclical pattern to which I have referred, and by contrast some theologians have suggested that the biblical pattern is linear. But if I may say so, this is not right. If it was truly a linear pattern then we would certainly have no part in the final victory of God's purpose. It really is not something that can be described in geometrical terms, but only personal terms. There is no direct road from the here and now to the kingdom of God. The path winds down into the valley, reaching into the depths of desolation that Jesus alone knew. Only from out of those depths – of the crucified, humiliated and defeated Jesus – does God raise up the new creation.

The resurrection of Jesus, from the degradation and defeat of the grave, is the pledge that out of the ruins of all that we bring about in history, God will raise a new creation. 'A new heaven and a new earth … for the old order of things has passed away' (Revelation 21:1, 4). There is no straight line. If you want a geometrical pattern, it goes right down. And only then, when God raises it up, does it reach its climax.

Basically, I am saying that geometrical patterns will not work. It is a personal relationship. Our actions are to be understood as acted prayers for the kingdom. We offer not just prayer but action. We offer ourselves to God. And because there is only one perfect sacrifice, that of Jesus on the cross, it follows that those actions which will be accepted, honoured and raised up by God, will be those we undertake for the sake, and as members of, the body of Christ – acted prayers through Jesus Christ our Lord. That is the model we must adopt in order to understand the relationship between our actions now and their connection to the end of all things.

There is that wonderful story of Jeremiah as he lay in prison (Jeremiah 32). One of his relatives came and told him that a piece of family property was up for sale and he ought to buy it. This land was under enemy occupation and the Babylonian armies were about to take and destroy Jerusalem and carry its people into captivity. Nevertheless, Jeremiah paid seventeen shekels of silver for it and then he asked himself the question we have all asked at times in our life, 'Why did I do such a stupid thing?' God answered him that in the end the land would be redeemed. Jeremiah took a risk which in relation to his current situation was seemingly absurd. But it was the action that corresponded to what God had promised. In fact it was the model for all our action, then and now.

Even in situations which seem hopeless, when acts of love, forgiveness or kindness seem irrelevant, we still undertake those actions. This is not because we think these acts are going to be immediately effective in some way, but because they correspond to what God has promised. They are therefore realistic actions corresponding to the ultimate reality, and are accordingly acted prayers for the kingdom of God.

I return to my question: What is it we see when we look forward? It is not merely an indefinite and unknowable future, but an advent. He shall come again in glory to judge the living and the dead. He will come again and he will come as Judge. If there is no final judgment, then the words 'right' and 'wrong' have no meaning. If in the end 'right' and 'wrong' add up to the same thing then they are meaningless words. Morality is reduced to my personal chosen values. But we cannot eliminate this word 'judgment' from our thinking: '… he is the one whom God appointed as judge of the living and the dead' (Acts 10:42). The reason for that is that he is 'the light of the world'. St John's Gospel says, 'This is the verdict [judgment]: Light has come into the world, but people loved darkness instead of light because their deeds were evil' (John 3:19).

The essential point about light is that in its glare things are seen as they really are, and in the end everything will be seen as it really is. There will in the end be no confusion between right and wrong, between truth and lies. If we sidestep that central element of our faith then the words 'right' and 'wrong' become meaningless. When we assert that a thing is wrong, even if everybody denies it, what we are saying is that in the end, in the light of Jesus, it will be seen that it is wrong. Otherwise, the word is devoid of meaning.

When we speak about judgment, we must remember that in all of the parables of Jesus about the last judgment, the emphasis is on surprise. Those who thought that they were in suddenly find themselves out. And those who thought they were always doomed to be outside, find themselves in. 'So the last will be first, and the first will be last' (Matthew 20:16). All things are finally in God's hands and we are warned that judgment, and the time for it, belongs to God alone.

Our creed goes on, 'I believe in … the communion of saints, the forgiveness of sins, the resurrection of the body, and the life everlasting.' The New Testament says little about what must always be a tantalising mystery of what happens to the believers who die in the faith before the end has come. Where are they and what happens to them? The New Testament is very reticent about it. In the New Testament all the emphasis is on that final victory, the resurrection of the dead, the judgment, the kingdom and the glory and the new heavens and the new earth. But there are hints, especially in that wonderful passage in Hebrews 11 and 12 where they are spoken of as 'a cloud of witnesses' (Hebrews 12:1) that surround us, looking to Jesus, with us looking to Jesus and waiting for the day of his glory.

In our Protestant reaction against an excessive concern about those who have died in faith in the Roman Catholic Church, many of us have been insufficiently explicit about this. I think that the communion of the saints, those who have gone before us, are still surrounding us as 'a cloud of witnesses' looking to Jesus. I think this despite the fact that we know little of their state and the Scriptures do not say much about them. And we can rejoice in their communion. Remember them, thank God for them, as a regular and important part of our prayers. This has certainly become an increasingly important part of my own prayers.

The Scriptures teach us that the resurrection of the body is the end and not the pagan idea of the immortality of the soul. The scriptural idea of the resurrection of the body is part of the whole vision of new heavens and a new earth, a fresh creation in which all that God had purposed for the creation of the world and his human family is redeemed and consummated in his kingdom.

Finally, the life everlasting. This is the communion in the life of the blessed Trinity for which Jesus prays on the night of his passion, 'That they may be one, as we are one: I in them and you in me. May they be brought to complete unity' (John 17:23). This is the prayer that we are permitted to enter into and in which we may live forever in the glory, the joy and love of the triune God. This is something that passes our understanding and yet continually beckons us as the true goal of our being.

Time and again, the New Testament reminds us that in this interval of time between the resurrection and the second coming, there is given to us a foretaste of that joy: the presence of the Holy Spirit. This is the pledge, the first fruit, the *arrabon* – to use that ancient word of the kingdom – not the whole reality, but a real taste of that bliss and freedom, and of the glory that belongs to God. These things are given to us so that we may possess in the external world of history the fact of the resurrection, and in the life of our own souls the presence of the Spirit as the double pledge that in the end, God reigns. And to him be the praise.

PART THREE

FAITH IN A CHANGING WORLD

10 CHRISTIAN FAITH IN THE WORLD OF SCIENCE

The belief that science and religion are in conflict is so ingrained in the public mind that perhaps we should go back to the time when this point of view was first put forward, for it was not always so. The great discoverers and practitioners of modern science were Christian believers. But it was chiefly in the nineteenth century that some of the most godly, righteous and eminent people in Britain, and Europe generally, saw science replacing religion as the guide for governing society. Science would be the one avenue for reaching reliable truth upon which humanity could rely, now and in the future. There was a deliberate effort in many ways to proceed down that avenue of science.

We think especially of T. H. Huxley, one of the committed propagandists of the view that science would replace religion. We may recall the famous debate between Huxley and Bishop Wilberforce in Oxford on 30 June 1860 when the British Association for the Advancement of Science was in town. Seeking to score a point against Darwin's disciples, the Bishop of Oxford unwisely baited Huxley by enquiring whether he would prefer to think of himself descended from an ape on his grandfather's or grandmother's side. According to legend, Huxley replied to the provocation saying that he would rather have an ape for an ancestor than a bishop. Wilberforce was supposed to have been ignominiously put to flight. But recent research on the original minutes of that meeting show this version of events to be inaccurate, a complete caricature of what actually happened. Wilberforce was actually present not as a bishop but as a biologist and he made a number of important points which Huxley accepted.

However, it was Huxley's great triumph in getting the body of Charles Darwin buried in Westminster Abbey that signalled the start of a new and widely held confidence that science held the key to humanity's future. Part of that confidence lay in the idea of progress. I am told that St Pancras Railway Station in London was built to look like a cathedral precisely to make the point that it was in human progress that the future would lie.

It was an idea that developed in the eighteenth century but which was a carry-over from the biblical vision of history as a meaningful story, as distinct from the religions of Asia. History there was not seen as a significant story, but as an area of shadows and illusions. For a thousand years the Bible had taught Europe to see history as a continuing series of events suffused with meaning. And what happened in the eighteenth century was that this meaning of history was to be found not in our journey towards heaven but towards heaven on earth and a truly glorious future for humankind. Until about 1914 – at the time of the First World War – it was taken for granted that endless progress was the meaning of history and that science was its engine.

It was, of course, into that concept of progress that the idea of evolution fitted so neatly. When Darwin espoused the theory of natural selection by way of the survival of the fittest, this provided, what you might call, a mechanistic, mechanical interpretation of progress. The worldview that dominated the nineteenth century was that of a mechanistic picture. The world was conceived as a vast machine where the movement of atoms, governed by the theoretical laws of gravity and momentum, would provide an explanation for everything.

And so the theory of the survival of the fittest and natural selection provided a mechanical explanation for progress and that was translated into the social Darwinism of the nineteenth century, which in turn led to those social policies about which we now weep: the Poor Laws and all those other devices which ensured that by ruthless competition the weak would be eliminated and the strong would not only survive but succeed at the expense of another's failure. It is a comforting view of history because we are the survivors and consequently the most fitting and adaptable and therefore, by implication, the ultimate meaning of history. It is a most satisfactory, convenient and attractive way of understanding history.

Behind the nineteenth century stands the great Enlightenment of the late seventeenth and eighteenth centuries, the so-called 'Age of Reason' or the 'Age of Enlightenment'. After centuries of darkness, it was believed the light had begun to shine. Societies could now get rid of traditions, religions and superstition, and with the aid of science, see the world as it really was.

Two things influenced this dramatic intellectual conversion in eighteenth-century Europe. One was the legacy of the religious wars. For most of the seventeenth century the soil of Europe was soaked in the blood of Christians fighting one another over their interpretations of the biblical story. That experience made the intelligentsia of Europe sick of the whole business of religion. The second positive influence was the emergence of the new science of the seventeenth century, especially the science represented in the cosmology of Sir Isaac Newton, the English mathematician and physicist, whose work was the greatest single influence on theoretical physics until Einstein.

In contrast with the fanaticism of the religious wars, there now emerged a picture of reality that was entirely rational and comprehensible. Newton's laws seemed to have provided an explanation for everything, from the movement of the planets to the falling of an apple. It was an intelligible vision of reality requiring no faith, no divine revelation and no miracles. You could see how it worked if you put your mind to it; anybody could. Given a proper education, everyone could be united in this rational, clear interpretation of the human situation. This new era – the Enlightenment – carried the ideas, education, science, technology and the political institutions of Europe all over the world and from this flowed that great phenomenon called 'civilisation'. At that time one did not speak of different 'cultures' as we do now. The idea of 'cultures' in the sense of differing societies first appears in the English language in the late nineteenth century. Previously there were no different 'cultures', merely more, and less, civilised people; and the business of the civilised was to help the less civilised up that ladder. Essentially, civilisation was the acceptance of this rational and entirely clear understanding of the whole human condition provided by this new science.

So one views the past beyond the eighteenth century into the seventeenth where the birth of the new science occurs. And we come to the momentous question: Why? Science, after all, is only another word for perceived or believed knowledge. I shall return later to that point, but the idea that science is a different kind of knowledge, that it is an absolute knowing of a quite special quality, is the way this word is curiously understood in ordinary language.

Why did this happen in Western Europe, primarily Northern Europe, and not elsewhere? After all, the sciences of Greece, China, ancient Babylonia and the Arabs, were in most ways far ahead of anything in Western Europe. The Chinese had printing, the magnetic compass and explosives long before we had them. And the brilliant mathematics and astronomy of Ptolemy, of the early Greek astronomers, and of course of the Arabs, was far ahead of anything in Western Europe. So why did this kind of science develop in Western Europe and not in those more ancient and, in many ways, more advanced cultures? The answer is both complicated and fascinating.

To answer this question in its most simple terms, the ancient science of Greece was carried over into the Arab world and developed into the brilliant Arab civilisation of the tenth, eleventh and twelfth centuries. It was based on the philosophy of Aristotle, which saw the ultimate realities in terms of first cause and final cause, the thing that started the whole universe off and the purpose for which it existed. Everything else was to be deduced from that, so one begins with these fundamental metaphysical realities and deduce from them what must be the case.

But the other great strand in the Western world was the biblical strand because for more than a thousand years the Bible was the only book, for practical purposes, that Western Europe had. It was the biblical story that shaped the mind of Western Europe and made Europe a distinct society and not just a peninsula of Asia, which from a geographical point of view is what it is.

It was the coming through of the translation of the great Aristotelian classics and the ancient science of Euclid and the Greeks, those translations first into Arabic and then Latin in the twelfth century, which created those tremendous conditions that eventually produced the Renaissance. The biblical story had a different way of understanding the universe. The Bible gave us a picture of the world as something that was created but which at the same time was contingent.

Let me attempt to explain. The biblical picture of the world was that it was the creation of a rational God and therefore was in principle comprehensible to the rational mind. One of the first principles the early Christian theologians had against Aristotle was that because the universe was the work of a rational God, and because we have been given a reason which reflects the rationality of God, the universe was therefore comprehensible in principle.

Furthermore, and here there is the sharp distinction from Aristotle, because the universe was a creation and not an emanation – as Indian philosophy would say – people had to find out for themselves how the universe actually was. We cannot deduce the nature of the universe from our knowledge of God; we have actually to examine it and find out how it is and how it works.

Indian philosophy has seen the ultimate wisdom as something to be found by the mystical contemplation of God so that our mind and the mind of God are in tune with each other. But with the biblical basis one had to proceed in a different way. The universe, being a creation of God, had a relative independence, a relative autonomy. It was not just part of God. It was not simply an extension of God, but a separate distinct reality and therefore one had to find out for oneself how it worked. So there was the basis for the whole experimental method of science, which lay at the basis of the development of modern science.

We shall come back to that a little later in looking at some of the earlier origins of science. But it is most interesting that right back in the fifth and sixth centuries in the school of Athens, which was both the great centre of Greek science and the centre of the best Christian catechetical instruction, a Christian philosophy of science developed there which quite specifically contradicted Aristotle on some of these essential points.

I referred to the mechanistic view of the universe, which dominated the nineteenth century, but now in the twentieth century science speaks a different kind of language. Scientists write about the history of nature, which of course would be incomprehensible for Newton. The cosmos has a time arrow. The famous second law of thermodynamics, said to be one of the most unshakeable foundations of science, states that in a closed system there is an irreversible movement towards randomness. To give the simplest example of what that means; if you put a cup of hot coffee in a cold room, the coffee will get colder and the room will get slightly warmer and that process cannot be reversed unless you introduce a new element into the room, perhaps a gas cooker. Within a closed system everything runs down towards entropy, towards randomness and if the universe is a closed system, as Newton taught, then the second law of thermodynamics is the last word and the universe has a direction.

That is something quite contrary to the popular understanding of science in the nineteenth century. There is now no longer a mechanistic view of the universe. We do not have absolute space and time as with Newton. Since Einstein the only absolute is the speed of light and everything else – including space and time – is relative to the speed of light, which is the one constant.

Since the development of quantum physics we know that the universe is not something the observer simply looks at from outside, as Descartes taught. Instead, there is an interaction between the observer and the observed, so that in many ways the coherent, confident, clear mechanistic view of the universe which dominated nineteenth-century thought has been broken down.

We are now in an era, if I am not mistaken, when there is an increasing amount of scepticism about science. The book by journalist Brian Appleyard called *Understanding the Present: Science and the Soul of Modern Man* (1992) created a furore at the time. *The Times* laid on a big conference in London and many scientists went along and vilified him. But the essential thesis of his book was that while science had achieved marvels for the human race it had done something to the soul. It had made us something much less than we were. It had reduced us.

I think I am right in sensing a considerable amount of scepticism today. There is the feeling that science is primarily understood as a means to power rather than as a path to wisdom; after all, an enormous proportion of all the work of scientists in the world today, surely over 90 per cent of it, is done in the interests of developing either military or industrial power. Do people now think that science is a way to wisdom and will answer the questions of what things are worth doing? Or is there increasing scepticism, as shown by the last two annual meetings of the British Association for the Advancement of Science which started off on defensive notes? In 1993 they asked how more students could be persuaded to go into the science faculties in the universities because enrolment was falling off. In 1994's speech, the president urged: 'Science is a good thing. Please don't bash it.' And of course there is the whole development of things like astrology and the New Age, and all kinds of irrationality, flooding into our present society.

So we are now in a different position from that of the nineteenth century. If we return to that century and its attack on religion, we have to consider several ways where it can be shown that this attack was based upon misunderstanding. The mechanistic picture of the universe was a prime example of reductionism, of trying to explain things in terms of less than their full reality. The prime example of that would lie the project of the great French astronomer Laplace, a contemporary of Napoleon. We are often told the story of Laplace presenting his cosmology to Napoleon, who in turn said, 'I find that you have not made any mention of God in your cosmology'. Laplace replied, 'I had no need for that hypothesis.'

One of the most famous affirmations of Laplace was that if one could know the position and direction of movement of every atom in the universe one would know everything there was to know, including the entire future of the universe from here to infinity. Now that is an extreme statement of the mechanistic view. But, of course, it is absurd because the Laplacian mind which knew the position and direction of every atom in the universe would in fact know nothing except an enormously complicated mathematical equation – because to know the atoms of which a thing is made is not to know the thing itself.

To know the atoms of which a flower is made is not to know the flower. The idea that really to know a thing is to know the smallest parts which comprise it is an illusion. To know the smallest parts of which it is composed might be of valuable help in coming to know it, but we do not know it except as the total reality that it is.

A simple example would be to take the precise image the nineteenth century loved to take, the image of the machine. How does one know the fullness of what a machine is? A machine depends for its operation on the laws of mechanics and you can explain the breakdown of a machine by discovering a defect in its mechanism, but you cannot explain what a machine is by simply examining its mechanism. One does not know what a machine is unless one knows what it is for. To suppose that an understanding of its mechanics brings an understanding of the machine is absurd.

But one could carry this point further, both down and up – as we saw in Chapter 4. The mechanism of the machine depends upon the constitution of the metal parts of which it is made, which in turn depend upon the chemistry of its steel, brass and copper, and whatever else there is. But mechanics cannot be reduced to chemistry. Mechanics depends upon chemistry, but chemistry will not enable you to understand mechanics. Furthermore, the combinations of elements which form the chemicals that we deal with depend upon the atomic structure of the molecules which make up those materials.

But you cannot reduce chemistry to physics. The chemical formation of anything depends upon the structure of its atoms and sub-atomic particles, which is the field of physics. But chemistry cannot be reduced to physics nor can you eliminate physics for the sake of chemistry. Mechanics cannot be replaced by chemistry. And to take it a step further up, an animal is, from one point of view, a machine. Its movement depends upon the mechanical working of its bones and muscles, but you cannot reduce biology to mechanics. You may be able to explain the collapse of an animal by a mechanical failure in its bones, but you cannot explain an animal simply by understanding the mechanics of its physical structure. Reductionism is sometimes called 'nothing-buttery'. A flower is nothing but a collection of atoms. The mechanistic understanding of the universe is a prime example of reductionism. But that is still quite widely practised. The great biologist Francis Crick, who discovered the DNA molecule, said he hoped to reduce biology entirely to physics so that all biological functions will be understood in terms of their physical causes.

The case of the machine clarifies the point that you do not understand a machine simply by understanding the physical, chemical and mechanical elements which make its functioning possible. As stated earlier, you do not understand a machine unless you understand the purpose for which it exists; you may understand the causes that make it operate, but you cannot understand the purpose for which it exists. For that there is only one way: either to ask the designer of the machine to tell you or to ask someone who has been told by the designer of the machine and therefore knows how to use it. This is because purpose, until it is realised, is hidden in the mind of the one whose purpose it is and it is not available for inspection.

The great conviction of the Age of Enlightenment was that one could forget about traditions, religions, superstitions, revelations and the rest, and that simply by the observation of the facts and rational organisation of these facts, one could discover what was the case. To take a simple example, if you are walking along the road and find piles of cement and a cement mixer and people with bricks and so forth, you know something is being built. How do you discover what is being built? There are just two ways, and only two, to find out. One is to stand around in the street until the building is finished. You can then inspect it and conclude rationally that it is a school. The other is to ask the architect and he will tell you and you will have to believe him. In other words, revelation.

If we are talking about the cosmos rather than a school, then the first alternative is not available. We shall not be around when it is finished. So if this cosmos has any purpose there could be no way of knowing it unless the one whose purpose it is reveals it. And if you exclude divine revelation as a source of knowledge you have excluded in principle the possibility of any rational knowledge for the purpose of the universe.

The next consequence which flows from this is relevant to our situation. If you do not know the purpose for which a thing exists, the words 'good' or 'bad' cannot be used in relation to it. It might be good for one purpose but bad for another. When I was a boy there was a great Scout jamboree in Liverpool and about the same time a new substance had been unleashed on the world, said to be edible, called 'shredded wheat'. One day this shredded wheat was issued as rations for all the jamboree troops and after breakfast there was a complaint in the camp office from a representative of the Nigerian Scouts, who exclaimed, 'These pan scrubbers are no use!' If the purpose for which a thing exists is not known then there is no rational way in which it can be called 'good' or 'bad'. If there is no public doctrine about what the purpose of human life is, about what human beings are for, then there are no rational grounds on which you can say that some kinds of human behaviour are good and others bad. It is simply a matter of personal opinion.

That is one point that has to be made about the nineteenth-century mechanistic understanding of the universe. This leads to others. I have been talking about different levels of understanding where there is a hierarchy of levels with physics at the bottom going up through chemistry, mechanics, biology and sociology.

But there is one particular level that has a special significance for us and I can illustrate it in this way. If you are sitting in a room talking about Joe Bloggs and Joe Bloggs suddenly comes into the room, you know that you have to stop that conversation or else start a new one where you talk *to* Joe Bloggs and he has a chance of talking to you. There has to be a break because the way in which we know a person as distinct from knowing about a person, involves a different type of reasoning from the way in which we come to know a thing. In the case of knowing things, or knowing about a person who is not here, we of course use our reason to dissect, analyse and discuss. We are in control of the situation.

If we are trying to discover what makes a frog jump, we can put the frog on the table and dissect it and we are in total control of the situation. We put the questions and decide on the experiments, so we are in charge. But if we are trying to get to know a person, then we know that we are not in that situation. We have to use reason in another way and be prepared to listen and be questioned ourselves. We cannot determine for ourselves the course of the discussion. It is not entirely in our hands. It is a different kind of knowing.

As we pointed out in an earlier chapter, in many languages there are two words for these two kinds of knowing. In French it is *savoir* and *connaitre*. *Savoir* is to know about things, and *connaitre* is to know a person. In German the corresponding words are *wissen* and *kennen* but in English we have only the one word, but we know there are two different ways in which our minds work when we are in these differing situations.

A person can of course be the object of analytical examination. A neuro-surgeon may be said to get to know the patient on whom he operates in an intimate way but we know perfectly well that the way in which the surgeon comes to know the patient is quite different from the way a friend or a lover gets to know that same person. There are two ways of using reason in these two situations. Both have their proper place but must not be confused. If the cosmos embodies some purpose and that purpose is the purpose of the One who is its Creator and Sustainer – because otherwise it could not have any purpose – then there is only one way to know that purpose. And that would be by opening ourselves up to the possibility that the One whose purpose it is makes it known to us.

In talking about these levels of understanding, it is important to repeat the point that each has its own proper authority. Chemistry cannot take over physics and neither can mechanics take over chemistry, and so forth. Similarly the personal level of knowing cannot take over the impersonal way. Both have their necessary place and autonomy; they are not to be confused. But neither are they to be completely separated.

If we look at the actual way in which science works we know that it cannot begin its work except by acts of faith. One has to accept the given data and the scientific tradition in which one is apprenticed. As the great St Augustine said, 'I believe in order to understand.' Nothing can be understood without an initial act of faith. A later thinker, in more detail, explained: 'I believe, in order to act, and I act in order to understand.' But nothing is understood without an initial commitment of faith.

If one then proceeds to examine the way in which science really works, and here a lot has been written by philosophers of science in recent years, one sees how so much depends upon the faith commitment, the personal commitment, of the scientist to the task in hand. Science does not begin with a sort of clean slate as the Enlightenment proposed. The Enlightenment, or the Age of Reason, wanted to wipe the slate clean of the traditions of the past and start from the beginning with the facts.

One of the great pioneers of the rise of modern science was

Francis Bacon, who advised his contemporaries to forget the so-called 'universals' of medieval philosophy, the principles with which Aristotle began, and to collect facts. But Einstein said much later: 'What you call facts depends upon the theory that you bring to them.' There can be no recognition of any fact except on the basis of the way you have already learnt to understand the world. This involves the way you have learnt to use language, concepts, images and models – and the way you have been trained as a scientist to accept the scientific tradition of understanding.

But the important point about Bacon's movement, which has shaped all science since, was that he excluded the concept of purpose. Aristotle had sought to understand the world in terms of its initial and final causes: what started everything off and what its purpose was. Aristotle claimed that in understanding this, you understood the world.

Bacon eliminated the concept of purpose; he did not accept it as a category of explanation. He accepted the concept of cause. If the universe is to be understood entirely in terms of the cause-effect relationships which link one thing to another, then you can discover how it works and can interfere with its workings to make it work the way you want. In other words, purpose can be imposed upon it. But if the concept of purpose were to be excluded from the category of explanation then the consequent conclusion, in the memorable words of Bacon, would be: 'Knowledge is power.' Science becomes essentially a means for power, for intervening in the world of nature to make it serve humanity's purposes. But it excludes, in principle, the question: 'Were there purposes for which things existed before I began to impose my purposes upon them?'

Michael Polanyi, the Hungarian physical chemistry scientist (1891–1976) to whom I am very much indebted for all this, answers the question in this way: when we recognise a problem, we have an intuition of a pattern of harmony, beauty, coherence, order – that somewhere in this chaos there is a pattern out there and it summons us to find it. The scientist thus responds to a call from something beyond us. It is significant that at the heart of science itself, there is some extraordinary sense, even if it is not acknowledged, of the presence of something which is there before us.

Why do scientists talk of the love of truth? What does it mean? Does it not mean that there is some beloved and beautiful entity out there that calls us forward and summons us, even at the cost of great struggle, to find this hidden harmony and coherence? Indeed, without that passion, science would never have grown and survived. As we all know, committed scientists have spent their lives attempting to solve problems which have often led them into blind alleys. Many have wasted their lives on lost causes such as perpetual motion or the philosopher's stone. But science could not have proceeded without that personal, indomitable passion of the scientist to find that hidden and illusive reality.

Back, now, to that nineteenth-century attack on religion. Why did it happen? The idea that science is a special kind of knowledge distinct from our perceived knowledge, that science makes available to us a sort of truth more reliable than the truth available to us from the experiences of life, is an illusion. Science is not a separate kind of knowledge; it grows from our generalised knowledge. Science is the attempt to formalise knowledge, ideally in such a way that it can be expressed by mathematical equation. But the sum total of knowledge that can be so formulated is limited.

For example, a young child learns to ride a bicycle without falling off. But to understand the mathematical formula involved in knowing how to turn the wheel of the bicycle at exactly the right angle to avoid falling off is irrelevant. The mathematical physics is irrelevant. A child can ride a bicycle by learning an unconscious technique which has nothing to do with learning a mathematical formula. There are vast areas of life where we know an enormous amount more than can ever be expressed in a precise mathematical formula, so that one of the great illusions that lay behind that attack was the idea that science was a separate kind of knowing. It is not. It is a part of a much wider area, what Polanyi calls 'tacit' knowing.

I was reminded of this when I had to register the loss of my suitcase at an airport in London. I had to report its exact description.

I found it extremely difficult to do so in a way that anybody else would recognise it. If my suitcase had arrived among two hundred other bags on the carousel, I would have known it immediately. But I cannot express all that knowledge with the precision of a scientific definition.

That would be an illusion. Only a small part of our knowledge can be so expressed, and science is simply part of our total understanding. The separation on our university campuses of the science faculties, against the other faculties, as though they were a quite different kind of human knowing, is based upon an illusion. But it is an illusion which has had undesirable consequences for our culture.

So the position is now very different from that of the nineteenth century. We now face an attack upon science, the growing irrationality of our world and the enormous popularity of astrology. It seems that no popular newspaper can succeed without a section on astrology. The growth of the New Age movement, while it encompasses elements of good, contains a vast amount of irrationality. Go into any bookshop today and ask for something on theology and you will often be directed to a section on the occult. This is common. I think that so far from having to defend religion from the attacks of science, the task of the church in the twenty-first century is going to be to reaffirm the foundations of science so that we may be saved from the floods of irrationality pouring over us. In the past, after the sixth century, for example, science was almost obliterated. It could happen again.

That recurring phrase in the Old Testament is good to go back to: 'The fear of the Lord is the beginning of wisdom.' Much Old Testament literature is called wisdom literature by scholars. It occurs in Proverbs, Job, Ecclesiastes, and so on. Much of it is common sense from the wisdom traditions of Egypt and other countries surrounding Israel. There is much we can learn by common sense. But occasionally in that wisdom literature this sentence is thrown in: 'The fear of the Lord is the beginning of wisdom.' If the ultimate reality which lies behind all the experience of this cosmos that we have, is a personal reality, God, not only the Creator of the world but the One who is constantly calling us to an increasingly deeper understanding of it – then the heart of the search for truth will be the fear of the Lord.

I always return to that wonderful piece in Job 28 where there is a description of the marvels of human technology. There is that picture of the miner working in the depths to extract gold and precious minerals from the earth with great descriptions of technology – and then: 'But where shall wisdom be found?' And then come the words: 'The fear of the Lord is the beginning of wisdom.' If that is so then we must accept that one of the immense tasks of the church in the twenty-first century will be to affirm the validity of science against those who attack it. And to remind the generations to come that it is the fear of the Lord that is the beginning, and end, of wisdom.

11 CHRISTIAN FAITH AMONG THE WORLD RELIGIONS

From the outset of his ministry St Paul acted decisively in his belief that the true interpretation of God's covenant with Israel was that the God of Abraham was to be the God of all nations.

The original promise to Abraham was that in him all nations should be blessed. Israel was called upon to be the servant of the Lord, the servant who suffered and would bring the gospel, the covenant, to all nations. This servant would gather them all together to be the people of the God of Abraham, and of Isaac and Jacob, and would act so that this would come to pass.

All the nations would be gathered together to be the people of the God of Abraham, and the hope of Israel would thus be fulfilled in this new community created by God. That was the essence of the message St Paul took to the synagogues of Asia and Europe.

Judaism, of course, is the religion of those who have not accepted that message. Judaism is a post-Christian phenomenon. And when that terrible time came after the destruction of Jerusalem, what would remain? Jesus had frequently foretold this destruction: 'If you do not repent, God will take away the vineyard from you.'

When this terrible thing happened, for those who did not accept the Christian interpretation of the story of Israel, what was left?

No Holy Land, no Temple, no sacrifice and no priesthood. All that remained were the people and the Book – the scattered people and the Book. So after the fall of Jerusalem the Jewish scholars gathered to establish the canon, the sacred fixed canon of what we call the Old Testament and what Jews call the Law, the Prophets and the Writings.

The Book was the centre around which the nation could be sustained. That is why for Judaism today it is of such vital importance that the Jewish race is preserved, that Jews are not lost by cultural assimilation through inter-marriage into the Gentile society, which is Europe.

So the heart of Judaism is the faith that God will eventually vindicate himself. And the way this can be assured is by preserving the distinct ethnic community of Israel and the faithful study and observance of the Scriptures. But there is, of course, one important strand in Judaism which says that God must vindicate himself by restoring his people to the Promised Land: the Zionist segment of Judaism has sought to realise the promise in the formation of the state of Israel in the twentieth century.

The third religion of the Book is Islam. In the Koran there are many references to the Old Testament and to Jesus, who is regarded as the last of God's messengers before the coming of the prophet himself. There were strong Christian and Jewish communities in South-West Arabia at the time of the prophet's life.

Unfortunately, there was no Arabic translation of the New Testament so while Mohammed had some knowledge of Judaism and Christianity, it was patchy and at some points inaccurate. But Islam shares with Judaism and Christianity the conviction that the kingdom of God must finally rule. 'Islam' means 'submission' and at the heart of the faith of Islam is the affirmation that there is one God and that all must finally come under his rule, as laid down in the Koran, the Sharia and the hadith.

From the very beginning Islam has been a religion of conquest. When Islam was born in the great battle which led to the capture of Mecca, the peoples of South-West Arabia had to the north of them the great Persian empire and to the west the great Roman empire, what we now call the Byzantine empire, which was a Christian theocracy. No doubt Islam was shaped to a considerable degree by what it saw in the Byzantine Eastern empire, the Christian empire.

Immediately after this great victory at Mecca, the armies of Arabia rode out on their camels to bring these two great empires under the rule of Allah, of God. It is one of the most amazing stories of history that within a century those camel-riding Arabs had destroyed two mighty empires. They had wiped out the Christian civilisations of the Middle East and North Africa and their armies had penetrated the heart of France.

It was an amazing triumph of a new faith, which nothing in history has quite matched. But at its heart and from the very beginning it was the faith of a people who believed that the power of the sword must finally establish the kingdom of God. Perhaps one of the most significant ways to emphasise the distinction between Christianity and Islam is to remember that at the decisive moment of his ministry the prophet rode into Jerusalem on a horse with a sword, to conquer, and at the critical moment of his ministry Jesus rode into Jerusalem on a donkey, to die.

But God forgive us, we have constantly forgotten those facts. We know that Christianity has also taken up the sword and been humiliated by doing so. But the fact remains that at the heart of these two faiths, both of which are rooted in the Bible, there is this profound difference between the way God's will was to be done on earth, as it is in heaven.

The next great world religion, and you might be surprised that I call it a religion, was that secular faith of 'modernity' or 'modernisation' which arose in Europe in the seventeenth and eighteenth centuries, which in the nineteenth century controlled Europe and led to the vast expansion of Western Europe into the rest of the world.

I call it a religion because modernisation functioned in the traditional way of religions. It dominated the understanding of reality and marginalised Christianity, and all other religions, allowing them only a small place in the private and personal lives of individuals. So the public life of nations came to be controlled by a comprehensive understanding of reality which one could conveniently sum up with the term 'modernity'.

Again, there are roots in the Bible. This new understanding of reality was a product of Western Christendom: it could not have arisen from one of the Asian cultures. Its biblical roots affirmed that history had a real meaning, that it was going somewhere, and was not just an endless series of cycles.

The difference was that the meaning of history in the Bible was to be comprehended by understanding the acts of God, but in this new faith that meaning was to be understood in terms of the actions of people. Human power, skill, civilisation, science and technology – these attributes would master the world and lead to the proper consummation of history.

In the twentieth century this faith expressed itself in two forms: Marxism and liberal free market capitalism. Of the two, Marxism is the closer to the Bible because Marx was a Jew who had a theological training. One can see clearly in Marx the influence of that biblical background. The ideas of freedom and liberation from slavery occur as the central themes of history together with this notion of a messianic people, a chosen people, who would become the agents of liberation.

Obviously it was neither Israel nor the church that would fulfil that task. The messianic people would be the proletariat – the workers. And finally, as in the Bible, the struggle between these two powers, of oppression and the oppressed, would reach a climax, an apocalyptic outcome, when the final battle would be fought and after that, freedom would be achieved. This Marxist picture dominated much of the twentieth century, but as we know, in its public, political form, it has now collapsed.

The other is the liberal free market, with its central idea of individual freedom from any kind of limitation, not human submission to God, as in Islam, but human freedom basically to do what we want. It is freedom defined negatively rather than positively. That is the fundamental point.

One can define freedom negatively as freedom from limitation, so that one is not constrained by any power external to oneself. In that sense the ultimate example of such freedom would be an astronaut floating in space having lost contact with the spaceship. That unfortunate person would be free of any constraint whatever, but would be incapable of doing anything, because one can only act if limitations are accepted.

Freedom defined positively, as the freedom to accomplish something, is wholly different. But our Western culture defines freedom negatively as freedom from limitation. Its centrepiece is the concept of the free market, that every individual is entitled to be free, without constraint, to get as much as possible for as little expenditure of labour as possible – often at the expense of another, or at the expense of another's freedom.

I know perfectly well, of course, that the free market is a good servant. It is the best way of continually balancing supply and demand in a changing world. But the free market is a bad master. When it is treated as the ultimate power, as it is in our Western culture, and when it is assumed that not even governments can control the markets, that these markets ultimately decide human destiny, then we are in danger of economic, social and moral slavery. We will have handed ourselves over to what Paul calls 'the principalities and powers', to the irrational forces which in many ways can enslave us, as indeed they do.

The difficulty is that essentially the Christian church has allowed itself to be domesticated into this religion of modernity. It has tried to accommodate itself at every point to what was called 'modern thought' and has effectively become incapable of challenging this false religion. Consequently a collapse of confidence also occurred which overwhelmed the whole project of modernity, leading to a picture of society completely unimaginable to our Victorian forebears.

We know with what supreme confidence they went throughout the world, completely convinced that Christian civilisation was the world's future. Today the picture is totally different. There is now a sense of guilt, apology and diffidence. And the church, because it was so closely identified with modernity, has suffered a similar loss of confidence.

So firstly we have the religions of Asia, secondly the religions of the Book – Christianity, Judaism, Islam – and thirdly the 'religion' of modernity, which in many ways is now the most powerful. The church is awakening slowly to the fact that modernity is the most powerful enemy it has faced in its two thousand years of history. This fact is made obvious when we consider that in the rest of the world the church is now growing faster than ever, but in those parts of the world where modernisation has taken over, the church is in retreat.

The next group are now known as the primal religions. They were once called the primitive or tribal religions. They are what might be called the natural religions of simple tribal peoples of Australia, Africa, the American continents and many village people in India, with whom I have spent most of my ministry, who do not know much about what we call Hinduism but whose religion is similar to the tribal religions of Africa.

Here, there is a universal sense of the presence of God, a god vaguely understood and without a clear personality. There is a sense that he is everywhere, that he is present in the trees, rivers and mountains. He is intimately tied up with the affairs of the tribe and there is a continuity between the present generation and its ancestors, of whom the ultimate ancestor is God and there is, in contrast to the religions of Asia, a profound sense of mutual responsibility.

The tribe has a cohesion, which leads to this strong sense of mutual responsibility. In this sense the tribal religions are in some ways much closer to the Bible than the religions of Asia, which ultimately are so individualistic. It has always seemed to me puzzling why we call them 'lower religions' and why we call the religions of Asia 'higher religions'. Perhaps part of the reason is that these tribal religions have no written scriptures. But that is not a legitimate basis for classifying them as 'lower'.

What conclusions can we draw from this brief survey? The first is that God has not left himself without witness anywhere. Every language in the world has a word for God. In some languages there is a sense of the reality of God being everywhere, but often without clarity or distinctness. And because in those languages God does not have a distinct character he is worshipped under many different names.

One of the most basic texts of Hinduism occurs in the Veda: 'Reality has many names, the wise know that it is one.' There are many names and many different characters; there is something there but it is not clearly known; it has no clearly marked character and therefore you have the pluralism of the world as we know it. This ought not to surprise us when we remember that the early church was launched into a pluralist world. As Paul said to the Corinthians, ' ... there are many "lords" and many "gods"' (1 Corinthians 8:5). That was the world into which the early church was born.

The historian Edward Gibbon put it quite neatly in his great work *The Decline and Fall of the Roman Empire*. Of that Roman world, he stated: 'All the religions were for the people, equally true; for the philosophers, equally false; and for the government, equally useful.' This is a nice succinct way of putting it.

Roman law tolerated that plurality of religions. There was a distinction drawn in law between what was called the public cult and the private cult: *cultus privatus, cultus publicus*. The private cults, of which there were an immense number, many of them coming from Asia, were ways of personal salvation through various kinds of discipline, mystical experience or ascetic practices. They were religions of personal salvation and the Roman empire made no difficulties for them. And if the church had been content to be simply a religion of personal salvation it would have had no trouble with the Roman empire.

But there was a sharp distinction between these and the public cult, which was expressed by the worship of the emperor. This was a specific act of worship. It would involve a little pinch of incense and bowing down in front of the statue of the emperor, one of which stood in every major city. As we know, the Christians refused that act and were ready to die for it. They could not, and would not, compromise on the question, 'Who is Lord?' To accept the title of Lord for the Roman emperor was impossible and the church was prepared to pay the ultimate price.

This new message, the gospel, then came into that Hellenistic classical world. But let us remember that this is about the gospel, not Christianity. It is important to make that distinction. The gospel is the story of what God has done in Jesus Christ, of his incarnation, ministry, death, resurrection and ascension with the promise of his coming again. That is the gospel. It is a factual story about what God has done.

As the first letter of John (v.l) says, it is about 'what we have seen and heard and touched'. It is about facts in that sense. I know it can only be understood in the context of the whole Bible and that the whole Bible can only be understood with this as the key, but the essential point is that it is a factual account of what God has done.

Christianity is what we have made of it – and we have often made a mess of it. Christianity, as a religion among the religions of the world, is a changing and variant entity; it has both good and bad in its history, including some very dark passages. So this is not about Christianity but about the gospel, which is that by which Christianity must always be tested. And when that gospel came into that pluralistic world, what were they to make of it? What could they do with it? Of course, they could disbelieve it; and a vast number did.

But if it is accepted as true, if it really is true that Almighty God has done those things that we repeat in the creed and in our hymns, if what we read from Colossians 1 is true, then it must be part of a governing principle. If it is true that in Jesus Christ, the very power that created and controls the universe, is present here as part of our history and is not an unknown God, but one whom we can know and love and follow, if all that is true, then it cannot be something that fits into existing worldviews. It cannot be slotted in; it cannot be just an article in an encyclopaedia based upon other principles.

It has to be the governing principle which shapes absolutely everything else.

Take the great controversy between Arius and Athanasius. Arius wanted to fit the gospel into what everybody took to be the facts. The 'facts' are that God is other than the human world and therefore Jesus cannot be God – he must be like God. There was the famous controversy between *homoiousios*, of a like substance, and *homoousios*, of the same substance, which is what we repeat in our creed – 'Of one substance with the Father' – and some people have scoffed at the great battle fought over a diphthong, over '*o*' as against '*oo*'. But many of the great battles of the world have been fought on a narrow point, because it was a crucial point.

G. K. Chesterton illustrated this in an appropriate way when he wrote of a little girl away from home in bed at night, crying for her mother, and a lady goes to her and says, 'I am very like your mother.' But that does not help.

Is it really the presence of God or is it just very much like God? If it is the presence of God then all our ideas, beginning with what we understand by the word 'God', have to be completely recast and rethought, and that was the tremendous struggle for the church of the early centuries. What would recasting now mean in our science and knowledge and in our political and economic practices in this multi-religious area? But that is another topic.

I shall conclude with a number of points about what I think this should mean for our practice. First, our relationship with people of other faiths must be to remember that they are made in the image of God. The same light that lightens everyone shines upon us all. There is no human being in whom there is not some witness to the truth of God, some evidence of the grace of God.

Therefore our first approach must be to seek out, to welcome, to cherish, to rejoice in the good that we find in a Hindu, a Muslim or a Marxist, or whatever, and not to take the other line: 'Well, this fellow is a Hindu so there must be something wrong with him – let's find out what it is', and then go on to winkle out his sins, so that we can talk to him about salvation.

That approach is completely wrong. The first thing we must do is to thank God for whatever good there is in a person of another faith.

The second is that we still have a story to tell. I like the wonderful story in Acts 10 of that pagan Roman centurion. We read, you remember, that an angel of God told this pagan soldier that his prayers and offerings had been accepted by God. The angel did not go on to say, 'Okay, no problem.' He said, 'Send to Joppa for a man called Peter who will tell you something you need to know.' And Peter came and told quite simply the story of Jesus. And as he did so this whole company, the people who came with Peter and the household of Cornelius, were caught up into an experience of the Holy Spirit.

So we have both to affirm the goodness that is there already, by the grace of God, but also to tell the story that is entrusted to us. Of course, we are not worthy to tell it, but if we do not tell it, then nobody else will. We are all entrusted with that story.

I was once at a meeting when a distinguished and able lady blasted off about the church. She said it was a hopeless institution with absolutely nothing worth looking for in it. If you wanted new and interesting ideas you had to find them elsewhere – and never in the church. And the man sitting next to me, Professor Nicholas Lash of Cambridge, just quietly replied, 'But if we don't tell the story, who will?' We are entrusted with that story, the gospel, and we have to tell it.

The third point is that we are not the judges. We are entrusted with the story and we are witnesses, not to ourselves but to Jesus. We are not the judges. We have no authority to discern or decide in advance who is and who is not going to be saved. Allow me to enlarge upon that.

In all of the teachings of Jesus about the last things, the emphasis is on the element of surprise: 'The first will be last and the last will be first.' The people who thought they were in will find they are out; those who thought they were out will find they are in. The things that are going to be burned are not the thistles growing around the vine, but actually the branches of the vine that do not bear fruit. We have to be prepared for surprises.

Then there is the whole debate about inter-faith relations, which has in my mind been radically poisoned by making a central issue of the question, 'Who is going to be saved?' So we have the famous classification of 'exclusivists' who believe that only Christians will be saved – and then you have to decide who is a real or a nominal Christian. On the other hand the 'inclusivists' say other people will be saved but only through Christ, while the 'pluralists' maintain that everybody will be saved whichever way they go.

None of these is a possible or tenable position. My view is that if it is true that God has done what the gospel tells us he has done, the question of who is going to be saved does not arise. The questions should be: 'How shall God be glorified? How shall he be thanked?' My understanding is that the whole mission of the church is the glorifying both of God and the name of Jesus.

The whole emphasis should not be on me and my salvation, nor on his or hers, but on God and his glory. Quite simply, the final salvation of other people is God's business. Remember, when somebody asked Jesus, 'Are there few that are saved?' Jesus replied, 'You try to go in by the narrow gate because there is a broad way that leads to destruction and many go that way.' Salvation is in God's hands. We have the responsibility of following Jesus along that straight and narrow way.

The fourth point is that there is no spectators' gallery, no non-committed point of view from which we can judge our different positions. And I return to the proposition that if you seek to justify your faith in Jesus in conversation with people of other faiths by resting upon some other grounds, some philosophical or historical grounds, you are in fact selling the past.

In the end we simply have to introduce people to Jesus and tell the story of what God has done. But even that is not the last word. I have often been pressed by Hindu friends who ask, 'Why do you insist on Jesus only? Why can't you recognise that Jesus is only one, perhaps even the greatest of all the great souls that have lived in the world? Why can't you accept that?'

At the end of the day, I can only say because God has called me in ways that I cannot fully understand. God has called me to be a witness for Jesus Christ, and I must bear my witness.

So I fall back on the words of Jesus: 'You did not choose me, I chose you' (John 15:16). 'I chose you.' That is why we are here. And that is the ultimate ground of our confidence as we bear witness to Jesus as Lord.

12 THE GOSPEL IN THE PUBLIC SQUARE

In this final chapter, let us consider what part the gospel of the church has played in the public square – in the civic, political and economic life of society. The church once dominated the public square: the very architecture of such places demonstrates this fact.

The nineteenth century was a time of vigorous movement affirming that science now provided the guidance society needed while religion was relegated to the level of private personal opinion.

When we say that the gospel is truth, that it is therefore public truth, the truth that ought to govern all our lives, public or private, does that mean or imply, for example, that the church ought to seek to recover the kind of role that it had in the Middle Ages or in the Byzantine world of the first millennium?

Perhaps the first approach would be to look briefly at the ministry of Jesus and the relationship of his earthly ministry to the worldly powers. The first thing to be said is that Jesus obviously did not seek to control the world.

That was one of the temptations he faced in the wilderness. The devil's questions, when he tried to tempt Jesus in various ways, are graphically described in the Gospels of Matthew and Luke: 'If you are the Son of God, what are you going to do? How are you going to bring in the kingdom of God?' These temptations, including those typical of worldly power, to provide food and demonstrate spectacular examples of power and so forth, were refused by Jesus, who then went unarmed to his ministry. That is the first point.

Then secondly there was Jesus in his teaching. He constantly warned the holders of power that their paths were leading to destruction. He could use harsh words when necessary. When somebody brought word from Herod that the king sought to destroy him, Jesus replied, 'Go tell that fox, "I will drive out demons and heal people today and tomorrow, and on the third day I will reach my goal"' (Luke 13:32).

Jesus repeatedly warned the holders of power in those times that unless they repented, their nation would be destroyed. And we know with what agony he gave that warning: 'O Jerusalem, Jerusalem, if you had known the things that belong to your peace, but now your house is left to you desolate' (Matthew 23:37–38 paraphrased). That terrible warning was fulfilled forty years later when the Romans wiped out the Jewish nation.

Thirdly, in the trial of Jesus before Pontius Pilate we see that Jesus acknowledged Pilate's authority over him because that authority was granted by God. Jesus accepted the power and authority of Pilate as given to him by the Father, but adds: '… the one who handed me over to you is guilty of a greater sin' (John 19:12). It is the abuse of that power and authority to create injustice which is the sin.

So three simple things could be said about Jesus: he did not seek worldly power; he warned those who held it that they were accountable to God; and, when he was being unjustly charged before a Roman governor, he acknowledged that the power and authority of Pilate was granted by the Father.

And so we come to this question: Who rules the public square? Who has the final authority? The Bible speaks about 'the ruler of this world'. There is much in the writings of St Paul, as we know, about principalities, powers, dominions, authorities and rulers (Ephesians 6:11ff). In the teachings of Jesus there is a great deal about 'the ruler of this world'. And remember the parable of Jesus about the strong man who was armed: only if a stronger man could overpower him would he be able to plunder his goods (Mark 3:26–27).

The coming of Jesus was the coming of the kingdom of God into this world. But the rulers of this world did not recognise him. As Paul said in his first letter to the Corinthians, 'None of the rulers of this age understood it, for if they had, they would not have crucified the Lord of glory' (1 Corinthians 2:8 paraphrased).

Those rulers – the principalities and powers – were people such as the priests and Pontius Pilate who between them represented the law and political authority. These were the representatives of 'the ruler of this world'.

And when we come to Romans 13, that famous chapter, where Paul said that all the established powers were ordained by God – 'ordained in order to reward the good and punish the wicked' – we find something of relevance to our times. They had an authority from God, they carried the sword; in other words they had the final power, and therefore it was the duty of all Christians to obey and pay taxes to them – something quite relevant to political discussions.

It is interesting to note that later in Romans 13 the Roman empire is described as 'God's minister to maintain justice and to punish the wicked' – and then compare that with Revelation 13 where the same Roman empire is portrayed as 'the beast out of the abyss' recognisable by the seven horns, the seven hills on which the city of Rome was built.

These are two completely different pictures of the political order. Something similar occurs in the first book of Samuel where the people complain that they want to have a king like other people, and not just have prophets. Samuel is told to tell them what a disaster kingship could be in the ways kings exercised their powers over people.

But then in chapter 9, the next chapter, God tells Samuel to go and anoint Saul as king. So there is this ambivalence about political power. On the one hand, it is established by God. God anoints

Saul. The political power and authority is ordained by God, says Romans 13. But on the other hand, political power and authority could become an instrument of demonic power.

How are we to understand this language of the New Testament where principalities, powers, dominions, rulers and authorities all play such a prominent part both in the Gospels and the Epistles? Let us consider what is said about them. In Colossians (1:15–20) we are told that all the principalities, powers, authorities and dominions were created in Christ and for Christ. They were therefore part of God's good purpose for the world.

But in Colossians 2 we find that in the cross, Christ disarmed the powers and made a public exhibition of them. He did not destroy them; he disarmed them. So in the cross, the powers, the political order and religious order, the moral law – all those things that were part of the powers – were found to be the enemies of the living God, which meant that they had been unmasked and shown up. They had, as Paul said, been disarmed. They were not destroyed; they still existed, and they still exist.

In Ephesians 6, we read that our wrestling is 'not against flesh and blood, but against the rulers, against the authorities, against the powers of this dark world' (v. 12) and so forth. So these powers are on the one hand created for a good purpose, but on the other, they can become instruments of evil. It is essentially the same point we saw in the answer Jesus gave to Pilate on the question of power and authority.

Let us take some examples of how the gospel stood in relation to those powers. Slavery was part of the economic order of the first-century Hellenistic world. It was as integral a part of their economy as usury is of ours. The Bible forbids usury – the taking of interest on loans (Nehemiah 5:15). In modern usage usury means the charging of iniquitous rates of interest, but the charging of reasonable rates is nevertheless integral to our own present economic system. So in a similar way slavery was an inescapable fact, and one that could not be abolished overnight.

How did the gospel stand in relation to slavery? On the one hand,

Paul said that in Christ there were neither slaves nor the free. The free were the slaves of Christ, and those who were slaves in society were the free sons and daughters of God. So in one sense, slavery was abolished within the church but in the economic order it still existed.

In chapter 5 we referred briefly to an almost perfect example of what this means in practice. In the little story contained in the letter to Philemon – that beautiful little letter at the end of the Pauline letters – there was a runaway slave called Onesimus. The name Onesimus means 'helpful'. Apparently he had defrauded his master, probably by stealing money (at least reading between the lines, that is what it looks like).

He came into contact with Paul and through Paul was brought to the Christian faith and became a believer. So what did Paul do with him? He did not urge him to run away and become a free man. Instead, he sent him back to his owner, but with that wonderful letter, one of the most beautiful pieces of literature in the whole Bible. Paul wrote, 'Formerly he was useless to you, but now he has become useful...' (Philemon v.11). The message continued, 'Now he is really what his name implies and I am sending him back to you in my place, as my representative, because I cannot come immediately. He is the one I am sending in my place' (vv.16–17 paraphrased). So Onesimus returned to his master, still a slave, but at the same time with the status of an apostolic 'nuncio'. He was the apostolic representative in the household of Philemon. This is a beautiful example of the relationship of the gospel to one of these powers.

We know it took a long time for the church to recognise that slavery must be completely abolished, not merely in the church. But there are many contemporary issues of a similar kind. We have to recognise the reality of these powers and structures of corporate life, which we cannot immediately abolish, and we have also to realise that they can become demonic.

Another very good example is race, which is a good thing in the sense that kinship and family ties are a good thing. Race is a kind of extended family. We are not all mutually interchangeable snooker balls. We exist as members of families and ethnic groups. This kind of bonding is a precious part of our being.

This was realised by English missionaries in South Africa who faced the issue of whether African converts were to be assimilated into English culture, as the Portuguese and the French had insisted, so that these converts should speak English and be part of English congregations. The English missionaries did not insist. These people would be free to have their own congregations where their own racial group could meet and worship in their own language; and that was good.

But when that understanding is made into an absolute that takes precedence over the unity that we all have in Christ, then it becomes an instrument of the devil. It becomes the sin of apartheid. So something which is good in itself, can become evil, an instrument of demonic power. One could give many similar examples.

We have been considering an economic order where slavery was integral to a society's economy, and you could no more immediately abolish it than we could wipe out interest rates in the societies of today. Yet the gospel introduced into that economic order something which must eventually radically transform it and lead to the point where slavery would become intolerable.

Now if we view the political order in Romans 13, we see the bald statement that the powers that be were ordained by God, and that in practice meant the Roman empire, so these powers were to be obeyed and taxes were to be paid.

But, as Paul said, that also meant that they were ordained for a certain purpose. This was to establish justice, punish the wicked and support the good. Accordingly, it became the duty of Christians to remind those powers of the one to whom they were responsible, and of the purpose for which they existed. One of the saddest things of our time is that the churches are so timid about doing this.

I shall always remember the time I was a student taking part in a great conference. Two thousand students were being addressed by that great Archbishop of Canterbury, William Temple, whose speech was being broadcast live on BBC radio. The news suddenly broke of government action, which was a flagrant breach of promise.

I have always remembered that moment. I was sitting in a gallery looking sideways at the archbishop when he suddenly abandoned his notes and spoke straight into the microphone, live on BBC, and proclaimed, 'The whole British people should rise up as one and say that a government which does this is not fit to exist for a day.'

We do not have many church leaders like that today, with the sort of courage to do that. But what he did was part of the duty of the church. This involves supporting the government, obeying laws passed by the elected government, paying taxes. That duty further involves constantly reminding the government of the purpose for which it exists. Governments must be reminded of the authority to which they are finally responsible – of the judgment seat before which they will finally stand.

And when political orders, governments of whatever kind, claim absolute power and authority for themselves, then they become the instruments of the devil. They become demonic.

To return to economics. Until perhaps the eighteenth century economics was regarded as a branch of ethics. It considered how one should behave in the getting and spending of money. It was a subordinate part of ethics, warning people against greed and covetousness and about fair wages and fair prices.

The medieval church tried, with considerable success, to ensure legislation was in place to provide for both fair wages and prices. The aim of economic life was not endless growth and the multiplying of goods and services beyond limit. It was to secure fairness, absence of covetousness and greed and the fair distribution of power.

The Old Testament prophets spoke vehemently against the unjust use of political wealth and in particular, of course, opposed the practice of usury, of taking interest on loans. And the medieval church sought to maintain that position.

The Jews, who by law were allowed to charge Gentiles interest, became the great early capitalists of the late medieval age because they could lend money on interest. But it was still regarded as contrary to clear biblical teaching that Christians should charge interest on loans.

It is interesting to note that even as late as Martin Luther, the German Protestant reformer who died in 1546, this prohibition on interest was absolutely maintained. John Calvin, the Genevan religious reformer who died in 1564, represented a more urban society and was prepared to agree that in some circumstances a modest charge of interest was legitimate for a Christian. But this whole arrangement was upset by the enormous and unprecedented inflation which followed the discovery of gold in the New World.

The vast quantities of available gold and silver, the two metals used for monetary exchange in Europe, sent prices rocketing and completely upset the whole attempted balance of wages and prices. The later exploitation of India and the Far East added to that explosive inflation so that the old medieval laws became unworkable.

But Christian preachers, right up to fairly recent times, still insisted that the economic life of a nation must be subject to biblical and Christian laws. But then we come to the Enlightenment, that Age of Reason in the late seventeenth and eighteenth centuries which eliminated divine revelation from the public sphere and taught that rational argument and rational calculation, not divine revelation or moral law, were the ways to guide economic life.

The great paradigm, the great model that controlled the thinking of the eighteenth century, was Sir Isaac Newton's model of the universe, which was seen as a vast mechanism where particles of matter in atomic form moved ceaselessly in accordance with the laws of gravity and momentum.

By this marvellous balance this vast cosmos, from the stars to the falling of an apple, was maintained – in accordance with those laws – in perpetual harmony and perpetual motion. That model captivated the mind of the eighteenth century. And it was inevitable that it would also be applied in other fields.

And so we have the work of Adam Smith, usually thought of as the father of modern economics. He developed the concept of capitalism, or the capitalist system, which would operate on a similar basis.

Society, according to this concept, consisted of an infinite number of atomic individuals who were moved, not by gravitation but by self-interest. Every human being was a unit of self-interest who therefore sought to gain as much wealth for as little labour as possible. There you have the human equivalent of the law of gravity. It was the continual interaction of those individuals in accordance with this mechanical system, which enabled society as a whole to flourish.

In the famous illustration that Smith gave, when the butcher provided you with good meat for your Sunday dinner it was not an act of philanthropy. He was not trying to serve you, but rather make a profit for himself, but in making that profit he served you. There was, as Smith said, an invisible hand which had so ordered human affairs that the operation of self-interest in a free market would bring the maximum good to everybody.

It is important to note, however, that before Smith started on that enterprise he was a moral philosopher. He made it clear in his writings in the eighteenth century that this system would only work for the good of society as a whole if society was permeated by moral sentiments. He was a moral philosopher and those sentiments would have to prevail in society if that system was to work with the perfection Newtonian physics ascribed to the cosmos.

When we move on to the late nineteenth century, the century when a deliberate attempt was made to suggest that science had replaced religion as the ultimate arbiter of the public square, we find the works of Alfred Marshall. He was the first economist to attempt to elevate economics into a self-standing science and detach it completely from morals and ethics. He affirmed that the free market system would operate automatically for the good of society without regard for moral sentiment.

When that idea was combined with the Darwinian theory of evolution, that the development of society, and the human race in particular, was the result of natural selection or the 'survival of the fittest' in a struggle for existence, then ultimately there would be a price to pay. This was called Social Darwinism.

The theoretical laws of economics were absolute and could not be tampered with. For example, when around one million Irish peasants died of starvation and disease in the mid-nineteenth-century potato famine, the economists and the British government both believed that charitable aid would interfere with those theoretical laws of economics. And that, they reasoned, would be disastrous. So up to a million people, out of a population of eight million, were allowed to die in the name of economic science. We are still paying the price.

In England children crawled through tunnels in coal mines, dragging coal carts. Chimney sweeps used small boys, street urchins, to climb and clean the internal chimneys of middle class houses. Any interference with those inhumane practices in the name of charity would have been condemned as ultimately harmful to the system. It would have interfered with the beneficent workings of the theory of economic law.

And so there occurs this great paradox, this irony, that at the precise time when Britain was becoming, and did become, the wealthiest nation in the world, the condition of its masses was that of a subhuman existence. The novels of Dickens vividly remind us of that fact. So *The Wealth of Nations* – to use here appropriately the title of Adam Smith's book – was to be built on the misery of human beings.

Consequently, at the end of the nineteenth century, the rise of Marxism occurred, which I believe was essentially an explosion of moral outrage against the injustices of capitalism. But because it was a nineteenth-century movement, it had to camouflage itself as a science. So we have this nonsense of economic science as understood in Marxist economics. But I am certain that fundamentally Marxism was an expression of moral outrage against the iniquities of the nineteenth century.

The collapse of Marxism as a world power in the past few years has created an entirely new situation where the free market operates on a global scale. With the enormously enhanced power of communication and efficient use of information made possible by modern computers, this global economic system operates increasingly as a self-governing entity, which has become a market that even the most powerful of governments cannot control.

It was a lady not accustomed to accepting dictation from higher powers who declared: 'You can't buck the market.' It was as if the world had been put on automatic pilot making the human pilot redundant. But the problem with the global economy is that we do not know its destination. An Indian bishop told me that Indian villages were being devastated by globalisation. The Indian government's change of policy, which opened up the whole of India to the free markets, has simply made India part of this global mechanism, and we are familiar with the consequences.

People are so much shaped and influenced by their own cultures that they often forget the fact that there are many societies in the world which are still what the economists call 'autonomous economies'. I have been familiar with them in my work among Indian villages.

By an autonomous economy I mean a largely self-sufficient society which has learnt to live within its own means. Such societies have very little trade or barter with the outside world. They have little need for money and have accepted a certain standard of living which they do not wish to change. These autonomous economies do not regard covetousness as a virtue but rather regard it a virtue to accept things as they are.

Obviously that is entirely subversive for the global economy. Indian villages are now being invaded by high-pressure advertising from global multi-national companies seeking to persuade people that they need things without which they have lived for thousands of years, and been quite content.

I remember once preaching in a little Anglican church in Geneva, a city which is one of the great centres of world capitalism. It happened to be the second Sunday in Lent when the collect for the day was a prayer that God would 'grant us the gift of godly abstinence'. I asked the congregation if they realised what they were doing when they offered that prayer, because if God answered it on a large scale the capitalist system would collapse.

But there are negative effects of globalisation, of a single free market. First there is the massive destruction of the environment, of which we have only become aware in the past forty years or so. It is extraordinary how recent that awareness is, dating from around the mid-1970s.

A book of futurology was first published in 1970 entitled *Future Shock*, by Alvin Toffler. It was widely read and commented upon. It professed to paint a picture of the world we could expect to see in the next hundred years or so.

It had, however, absolutely not one word to say about the environment. Later, after this book had become a bestseller, the report of the Club of Rome came out which warned us, for the first time, that we were exhausting the resources of the planet at a rate which could not be sustained. To put it in its simplest terms, if the globalisation of the free market should succeed to the point where all humanity had the standard of living that we have in the West, then the planet would become uninhabitable within a few decades.

The next unwelcome effect is that of polarisation between rich and poor – between nations and within nations. We have seen this demonstrated adequately in Britain during the nineteenth century. One of the simplest ways of making the point is to quote statistics published by the United Nations.

In 1960, the year of the 'development decade', when development became the key word in economics for the first time, it was reported that the richest one billion of the world's people had an income thirty times that of the poorest one billion. Thirty years later, after three decades of development, the factor had risen from thirty to one hundred and fifty.

Furthermore, this process of globalisation, of the free market, destroys the autonomous economies and inevitably results in mass migration from those previously autonomous villages into the enormous urban sprawls with which we are so familiar in places such as Calcutta and Bombay. In those cities no one really knows how many millions of people live on the streets.

The final result is what is called 'anomie', which we see everywhere in the so-called developed world. This loss of meaning and sense of purpose, this condition of hopelessness, is what drives people to seek immediate satisfaction in drugs or other forms of escape.

And in these circumstances the one global power that is challenging the dominance of the free market, now that Marxism has collapsed, is Islam. Its resurgence, as a global power, is now of prime importance in world affairs.

I believe it was the British Ambassador to Tehran who declared in 1979, after the Shah of Iran was deposed and replaced by Ayatollah Khomeini's Islamic Revolutionary Government: 'This event might, in world history, come to be recognised as equally significant with the French revolution of 1789 or the Russian revolution of 1917.'

That might, or might not, turn out to be true but there is no doubt that Islam is challenging globalisation. With its doctrine of the rule of the Sharia, the path to be followed in Muslim life, including economic life, Islam – which still accepts the prohibition of usury and proposes and seeks to operate a radically different economic order – is now challenging the supremacy of the global free market.

In doing so it is able to call upon the kind of groups to which Marxism once appealed – the poorest victims of the free market. So one finds that powerful Islamic movements are now being directed against those Arab countries such as Saudi Arabia and the Gulf states which have simply accepted the free market system. The political and religious ideology of Islam is now a major factor in international politics.

This broad sketch shows where we are and the road we have travelled. What can we say about the Christian response to all this in the field of economics? As I said of slavery in the first century, we cannot simply opt out of our world. We cannot simply remove those elements in society which are in conflict with God's will.

For us, just as it was with Paul and Onesimus, we have to recognise that we are part of this world and cannot simply migrate out of it. But at the same time we have to inject into it those things which will eventually transform it. And perhaps the first thing to be said is exactly the point I made about the collect for the second Sunday in Lent.

Is it not necessary that Christians should be explicit dissenters from the ideology of consumption? Should not Christians encourage others to disabuse themselves of the illusion that the goal of human life is increased production of goods and services, that increased gross national product is in itself a good thing? Is it not necessary that we should return to the basic biblical teaching which underlies that collect, that a godly abstinence, or to put it the other way round, that the cultivation of greed and covetousness, is incompatible with Christian discipleship?

Should we not recognise that we are most certainly on a collision course with a great part of our economic life? For we know perfectly well that almost all advertising in our culture is simply the attempt, by increasingly sophisticated means, to persuade us that we need things which we do not have and to encourage us in the culture of covetousness. It seems to me that at this point we have to be explicit and avowed dissenters.

We must do all we can to humanise the free market system. It is certainly not an evil in itself. The free market is the most efficient way of balancing supply and demand in a continually changing market. In that sense it is a good servant.

But when the free market is made absolute and we are told that it has the final word and that even the most powerful of governments cannot 'buck the free market' – when it is made into an absolute power – then we have to be frank and recognise that it is demonic and has fallen into the hands of the devil.

The free market as a servant is a God-given blessing, like all the other powers of which Paul spoke. But when it is made into an absolute, it becomes an instrument of demonic power. It seems to me that we must recognise that only the living God can confront demons; we in our own power are not able to do so. It is only the worship of the living God that can displace idolatry. It will not do simply to use moral arguments.

Part of our Christian discipleship, in which we acknowledge publicly that God and God alone is Lord, should be to use every influence available to humanise the free market system, just as Paul humanised, or began to humanise, the institution of slavery by sending Onesimus back to Philemon's household with the status of a representative of the apostle.

I am not sufficiently expert to go much further than that, except to suggest that there are certain steps that can be taken and advocated.

For example, the need to develop the whole system of auditing so that it is no longer simply a method of checking that all funds have been correctly used but becomes instead a means of estimating the real costs: the price that we are paying for what has been done, and is being done, to the environment and to societies.

Can we be ready to offer to our dying culture the framework of understanding that has its base in the gospel? If the gospel is to challenge the public life of our society, it will not be by forming a Christian political party. Transformation will take place by movements that begin with local congregations being faithful to a message which concerns the kingdom of God and his rule over all things and people. Such congregations, formed by the reality of the new creation, are thus called out by the Holy Spirit to claim every section of public life for Christ, exposing it to the illumination of the gospel and unmasking the hidden illusions of our secular society. It is time for the church to make the claim which it made in its earliest centuries, but which it vacated in the time of modernity, that it can provide the public truth by which society can be given coherence and direction.

We can be confident as we do this because God is faithful, he knows what he is doing, and he will complete what he has begun.

MORE ON
LESSLIE NEWBIGIN

If you have enjoyed this book, you may like to know more about Lesslie Newbigin and his work.

www.newbigin.net carries a searchable database containing a comprehensive list of this prolific author's writings and of substantial engagements with him. The site also contains the text (also searchable) of over fifty articles written by him.

www.gospel-culture.org.uk is the website of 'The Gospel and Our Culture Network' in Great Britain. This organisation was started by Lesslie Newbigin and its website contains a whole section on him, together with a complete archive of past newsletters including articles by him. The website also offers links to sister organisations in North America and New Zealand.

Paul Weston's book of selected extracts from Newbigin's writings is also available. *Lesslie Newbigin, Missionary Theologian: A Reader* was published in 2006 and is divided into two parts. Part One explores six foundational aspects of Newbigin's thought with extracts from his earlier writings, while Part Two uses later extracts to explore and illustrate his later writings in the areas of cross-cultural mission, inter-faith dialogue, the missionary crisis in the West, and the gospel as 'public truth'.

SPTC BOOKS

Holy Trinity Brompton launched St Paul's Theological Centre in 2005, following the growth of Alpha worldwide and the establishment of HTB as a major resourcing centre for other churches in the United Kingdom. SPTC continues to play a key role in the ministry of Alpha International and as developer of theological resources. In addition, in 2007 it became part of St Mellitus College, the newest theological college of the Church of England. St Mellitus is a pioneer in 'church-based' training, preparing students for ordination through a mixture of classroom learning and on the job church ministry. Working through Alpha International and St Mellitus, SPTC has sponsored a number of significant theological conferences, produced the popular Godpod podcast, and begun to plant branches around the world.

The central vision of SPTC is to help 'bring theology back to the heart of the church'. Rather than doing theology in a university or seminary setting, SPTC links its theology and its training as closely as possible to the life of the local church. The Centre is developing a rich seam of theological reflection on church life, following themes that arise from Christian ministry in churches like HTB and those who use the Alpha Course around the world. SPTC Books is an imprint of Alpha International, designed to help develop this theological work. It seeks to publish work linked in one way or another to the wider Alpha network, exploring theology in a way that is truly ecumenical. We will bring together the best of all kinds of theology from all parts of the church – all who are held together by a common belief in the God revealed in Jesus Christ and in the expectation of the presence and power of the Holy Spirit as the one who makes true worshipful theology possible.

ABOUT THE EDITOR

Paul Weston lectures in mission studies at Ridley Hall, Cambridge where he is an affiliated lecturer in the Cambridge University Divinity Faculty. He has taught at the HTB School of Theology and Chairs the UK 'Gospel and Our Culture' Network. He completed his PhD on Newbigin's later writings in 2001, and is the editor of *Lesslie Newbigin, Missionary Theologian: A Reader* (London/Grand Rapids, MI: SPCK/Eerdmans, 2006).